Twayne's English Authors Series

Sylvia E. Bowman, *Editor*

INDIANA UNIVERSITY

Anthony Burgess

(TEAS) 132

Anthony Burgess

By A. A. DeVITIS
Purdue University

ANTHONY BURGESS

Printed in U.S.A. by
NOBLE OFFSET PRINTERS, INC.
New York, N.Y. 10003

Preface

From the publication of *Time for a Tiger* in 1956 to *Enderby Outside* in 1968, Anthony Burgess's novels reveal an ever-growing competence as well as an ability to treat comically many aspects of contemporary society. His reputation today rests primarily on his ability to use the devices of contemporary "black comedy," but the so-called black aspects are, ultimately, the least significant aspect of his art. For Burgess is concerned with what all great satirists are concerned with—a betterment of the world so that men of sensitivity and goodness can live with dignity and pride.

In this study, intended primarily as an introduction to the artistry of Burgess, I have endeavored to relate the more extravagant aspects of "black comedy" to what I consider a fundamentally religious outlook. To do so, I have looked at what appears to be an "allegorical" approach to the problems that Burgess set himself in the individual pieces. I have examined characters, themes, situations, and symbols in order to suggest the subterranean meaning of the novels. Oftentimes I have neglected fascinating and compelling aspects in order to remain true to the introductory nature of this study. I hope that someone will do, thoroughly, some of the things that I have left undone: a study of the theological purport of many of the books; a full treatment of the satirical purpose behind the individual plots; a study of Burgess's use of language; and a study of the musical patterns that lie behind the novels. Within the next dozen or so years, as Burgess's reputation grows stronger—as it assuredly will—I am certain that many scholars will devote themselves not only to the problems I have outlined but to many more besides.

I should like to thank my colleague at Purdue University, Professor Allen Hayman, for reading portions of the manuscript with care and enthusiasm; Miss Sylvia Bowman, whose reading of the manuscript was both thorough and challenging; the Norton Company, for putting me in touch with Mr. Burgess and for

ANTHONY BURGESS

their editions of Mr. Burgess's works, which I used whenever possible; Mrs. Marie Skinner, who saw to it that a good deal of the early typing was done; Miss Sandy Barrett and Mrs. June Ogborn who did the final typing. But, most of all, I should like to thank Mr. Burgess, who, kindly and promptly, answered a number of questions that were perplexing me.

A. A. DeVitis

Lafayette, Indiana

Contents

Chronology

1917 Anthony Burgess born John Burgess Wilson, February 25, 1917, in Manchester, England.

1940 Graduated Manchester University, with honors.

1940- Military service.
1946

1942 Marriage to Llewela Isherwood Jones.

1946- Employed by Central Advisory Committee for Adult Educa-
1948 tion in the Armed Forces.

1948- Lecturer in phonetics for Ministry of Education, Preston,
1950 Lancashire.

1950- Employed at Banbury Grammar School, Oxfordshire.
1954

1954- Senior Lecturer in English, Malayan Teachers Training Col-
1957 lege, Khata Baru, Malaya.

1956 Publication of *Time for a Tiger,* the first installment of the *Malayan Trilogy;* entitled *The Long Day Wanes* in the United States.

1957- English-Language Specialist, Education Department, Brunei,
1960 Borneo.

1958 Publication, as John Burgess Wilson, of *English Literature: A Survey for Students; The Enemy in the Blanket,* the second installment of the *Malayan Trilogy.*

1959 Publication of *Beds in the East,* the third installment of the *Malayan Trilogy.*

1960 *The Right to an Answer; The Doctor Is Sick.*

1961 *Devil of a State; The Worm and the Ring; One Hand Clapping,* as Joseph Kell.

1962 *The Wanting Seed; A Clockwork Orange.*

1963 *Inside Mr. Enderby,* as Joseph Kell; *Honey for the Bears; The Novel Today,* British Council Pamphlet.

1964 *Language Made Plain; Nothing Like the Sun; The Eve of Saint Venus.*

1965 *Here Comes Everybody;* entitled *Re Joyce* in the United States.

1966 *Tremor of Intent; A Vision of Battlements.*

1967 Edition of James Joyce's *Finnegans Wake,* entitled *A Shorter Finnegans Wake; The Novel Now.*

1968 *Enderby Outside,* combined with *Inside Mr. Enderby* in the United States and called *Enderby; Urgent Copy.*

1970 *Shakespeare.*

CHAPTER 1

Introduction

IN a study of contemporary fiction entitled *The Novel Now*, Anthony Burgess makes strong claims for the future of the novel. "All I can say," he writes, "is that the novel is a form to which I am committed, that I am interested in the progress of the novel, that it is the only important literary form we have left and that I am proud to be involved in its continuing life and development."[1] Burgess came to the writing of serious fiction fairly late in life, for *Time for a Tiger,* his first published novel, appeared in 1956 when he was in his late thirties. The novel was the first part of a trilogy, one which he called *Malayan Trilogy* but which has been appropriately renamed *The Long Day Wanes* in the United States.

Before the appearance of *Time for a Tiger,* Burgess had devoted himself to serious music, writing chamber pieces, incidental music for plays, and large-scale orchestral works. In the introduction to *A Vision of Battlements,* the first novel which he actually wrote—although it was not published until 1965—Burgess tells his readers something about his musical compositions: "1948-49 had been, musically, a busy time for me. I had written various things for use—a piano sonata and a piano sonatina, a little concerto for piano duet and percussion, some realisations of Purcell songs, a polytonal suite for recorders, orchestral incidental music for *Murder in the Cathedral, The Ascent of F 6,* and *The Adding Machine*."[2] Burgess's first novel was undertaken not only to clear his mind of the burden of three years of army life on Gibraltar, where he served first as a sergeant and then as a sergeant-major in the British army, but also to satisfy a curiosity as to whether or not he could write an extended piece of prose without getting bored.

I *Various Writing*

Including the three novels that compose the Malayan trilogy, Burgess has written seventeen novels; two books of scholarly

11

import—one on language and one on James Joyce; a critical
survey of the modern novel entitled *The Novel Now*; and a
biography of Shakespeare. He has also edited an abridged
version of *Finnegans Wake*. He has, furthermore, written in-
numerable pieces, both scholarly and journalistic, for such
magazines and newspapers as *Encounter, The Listener, The
Hudson Review,* and *The New York Times Book Review*. In
1963 he began to write television reviews for *The Listener* on
a fairly regular basis; and in 1967 he undertook to write a letter
on the contemporary British scene for *The American Scholar*.
Similar letters also appeared in *The Hudson Review*. The letters
that have appeared in both of these periodicals reveal an ironic
as well as bemused attitude toward many aspects of English
life. For example, in the spring issue of *The American Scholar*
for 1967, he wrote: "It is not seemly to laugh, except very
bitterly, in the age of Vietnam and universal famine."[3] But his
descriptions of micro-miniskirted English girls and his account
of his setting out to sell reviewer's copies of the books he reviews
for magazines and newspapers are anything but bitter. In 1968
a volume entitled *Urgent Copy* appeared containing fifty-five
pieces of journalistic writing chosen from the various magazines
and periodicals to which they had been submitted originally.

II *Life and Backgrounds*

Born in Manchester, England, in 1917, Burgess, whose full
name is John Anthony Burgess Wilson, was educated first at
Xaverian College and then at Manchester University; his master's
thesis was a study of Christopher Marlowe. In 1940, he entered
the military, where he remained until 1946. In 1942, he married
Llewela Isherwood Jones, who died in March, 1968. When
Burgess remarried in 1968, his life took a new direction. *Life*[4]
magazine ran a multipage spread on Burgess in its October 25,
1968, issue; there, and later in *The New York Times*,[5] Burgess
announced that he was giving up residence in England. With
his wife Liliana and her son by a previous marriage, Burgess
left for residence in Malta: "It's not only to get away from
British taxes, although that's part of it. We [writers] are not
wanted here, you see. . . . We might as well get out. This is the
story of English letters today. It's all wrong. England used to
have wonderful writers. What a bloody shame. What a bloody

nuisance. Here we have to do journalism to live" (97). Burgess also announced that he was changing publishers, moving from William Heinemann to Jonathan Cape—suggesting, all in all, a new beginning. Newspapers and magazines soon announced, however, that the Malta adventure had fallen through and that Burgess was again on the move. More recently he has been living in the United States, in Chapel Hill, North Carolina, and in Princeton, New Jersey; lecturing in various parts of the country; and giving television interviews as he moves about.

More importantly, *The New York Times* for November 3, 1968, quoted Burgess's plans for future writing, plans which other accounts in newspapers and magazines have confirmed. Burgess told Anthony Lewis, his interviewer, that he was planning a novel on a Lévi-Strauss theme, "with the framework of an Algonquin legend about incest"; "a novel which will outdo, I hope, the French *anti-romancier*, the *nouvelle-vague* people"; and a parodic version of the *Divine Comedy*, to be written with his wife's help (60). His latest novel has been announced by Knopf for publication in the spring of 1971; it bears the provocative title of *MF*.

The *Times Saturday Review* of August 24, 1968[6] confirmed many of the points made by the popular press as to Burgess's plans but announced authoritatively that he was under contract to Warner Brothers-Seven Arts Studios to write the screenplay for a musical extravaganza based on Burgess's novel on the love life of Shakespeare entitled *Nothing Like the Sun*. The article went on to say that Burgess would work on the script, the music, and the lyrics. In November, 1969, however, gossip columns and trade papers published the information that Warner Brothers-Seven Arts was shelving a number of projects; and *Will* or *The Bawdy Bard*, Burgess's project, was listed among those discontinued. In June, 1970, announcements appeared in the newspapers concerning Stanley Kubrick's intention of filming *A Clockwork Orange*. Mr. Kubrick's concern, it seems, centered on whether to use the ending that appears in the first English edition of the novel or the one in the American edition.

III *The Problem of Audience*

The three years spent on Gibraltar, the scene of *A Vision of Battlements*, were important to Burgess for a number of reasons.

First of all, he decided to give up music—temporarily, perhaps, for he is constantly quoted as saying that he intends to return to it; second, emulating James Joyce, he tried his hand at novel writing, discovering the limits of his appeal as well as his ability to entertain; and, third, the army gave him a hierarchy against which to define his satirical talents. After his discharge, Burgess accepted a position for the Central Advisory Council on Army Education and then became a lecturer in phonetics in an English Training College. In 1954 he went to the Federation of Malaya, where he remained until the coming of independence. His first published works, which constitute the *Malayan Trilogy,* were intended primarily for a Malayan audience, for Burgess intended to become a Malayan citizen:

I addressed primarily an audience of English-speaking Malayans of all races—Malays, Chinese, Tamils, Eurasians, as well as expatriate settlers in the country; somewhere in the shadows I imagined a secondary audience of readers who had never been to Malaya. I assumed a knowledge of certain locutions, customs and habits of thoughts, and I did not attempt to explain them. I did not, for instance, say: "Malays, being Muslims, are allowed four wives" or "Friday is the Sabbath in Malaya." I regarded such information as dangerous, since it would imply a cold outsider's attitude and turn my characters into interesting foreign specimens, not creatures of the same flesh and blood as the ignorant reader. (*Novel Now,* 155)

Later, Burgess changed his mind and wrote for what he had originally designated as his "secondary audience." The locale and customs of the Malayan books occasion, of course, much difficulty for the Western reader, especially when the dictionary and the encyclopedia are of little help. A good deal of the humorous word play escapes the reader, who also feels at times that the intricacies and subtleties of racial relationships will forever evade him. But Burgess does succeed, and succeed superbly, in characterizing his people. He has said in a number of places that he never thought of the Malayan books as primarily comic but that they turned out to be comic anyway. The fact of the matter is that they are very funny, but their humor is only part of the truth that the books attempt to display. The introduction of an Occidental character or two does allow the reader to penetrate into the complexities of the background and to appreciate more fully the skill and dexterity with which Burgess exemplifies his themes.

Perhaps the most amazing aspect of Burgess's first three published novels is their uniform excellence. The reader remembers, of course, Evelyn Waugh's first brilliance in *Decline and Fall* and Graham Greene's marvelous competence in *The Man Within*. Burgess demonstrates comparable skill, and it is really unfair to point out as many of his reviewers do that he was a good deal older than Waugh or Greene when he published his first book. In the *Malayan Trilogy* the comic scenes are superbly built; and the human relationships and cross-relationships exemplified in and illustrated by the central character, Victor Crabbe, remain with the reader long after he has put the books down. Whether the reader has ever been to Malaya or not ultimately means little, primary or secondary audience notwithstanding, for Burgess's Malaya is as much a region of the imagination as geographical location.

In 1957, Burgess and his wife went to Brunei, a small but wealthy state in North Borneo, where he wrote *The Right to an Answer*, a novel that was very much admired by his early reviewers. Brunei also served as the locale of *Devil of a State*, called Dunia in the book. Three years later Burgess returned to England where, in rapid succession, he wrote fifteen or sixteen books. He appears somewhat sensitive about his prodigious output—some twenty books and several scores of reviews and articles in approximately fifteen years; but he points out with justifiable pride that writing is his craft and that many men of letters before him wrote large numbers of works.

IV *Art and Values*

As for religious beliefs and convictions, Burgess has written: "I was brought up a Catholic, became an agnostic, flirted with Islam, and now hold a position which may be termed Manichee— I believe the wrong god is temporarily ruling the world and that the true god has gone under. Thus I am a pessimist but believe the world has much solace to offer—love, food, music, the immense variety of race, language, literature, the pleasure of artistic creation."[7] Burgess's comments on the art of the novel also indicate his beliefs about the autonomy of the art object; but he concedes that no novel, however trivial, "can possess any vitality without an implied set of values from religion."[8] Since art is concerned with beauty—"a value which

we take as a representation of the Ultimate, under its aspect
of unity, formal harmony, Brunonian reconciliation of opposites"
—it is no wonder that Burgess approaches his craft with such
reverence.[9] In his many reviews of novels, Burgess is ever
ready to praise those who have been able to wrest so much
meaning from the stuff of human existence. "The organization
of words into meaningful patterns," he writes in *The Hudson
Review*, "it represents, against all odds, a sort of salvation."[10]

Burgess, then, regards himself as a serious novelist who in
his works is attempting to extend the range of subject matter
while exploiting words at the same time in much the same
fashion that the poet does. He acknowledges the influence of
James Joyce, Laurence Sterne, and Evelyn Waugh; but the
influences of Charles Dickens, George Orwell, Vladimir Nabokov,
and Aldous Huxley can also be found. Burgess admits furthermore to a real excitement in making the characters of his
invention move and talk as believable human beings, while
allowing them to express at the same time the intellectual thesis
that is the novel's essential reason of being ("Letter from England," 459). In the *Times Literary Supplement* for March 3,
1966, he writes: "Fiction can do little more than suggest that
the world is bigger than it looks and that it is in order to seek
a pattern in it. If it persuades us to meditate on life it is ful-
filling a sort of religious purpose. But its main aim is art, and
that is as should be" (154).

Speaking of his method of composition in *The American
Scholar*, Burgess characterizes it as "a very subtle and highly
organized mode of communication."[11] He uses very frequently
the musician's approach: in *The Listener* for May 3, 1962, he
indicates that Aldous Huxley showed in *Point Counter Point*
how musical concepts could be adapted to fiction: "I still think
that the novelist has much to learn from musical form: novels
in sonata-form, rondo-form, fugue-form are perfectly feasible.
There is much to be learnt also from mood-contrasts, tempo-
contrasts in music: the novelist can have his slow movements
and his scherzi. Music can also teach him to modulate, how
to recapitulate; the time for formal presentation of his theme,
the time for free fantasia."[12]

Indeed, consideration of Burgess's artistry in the novel requires
the critic to approach his works from many angles. Ultimately,
however, the fact remains that Burgess in at least seventeen

novels has attempted to "interpret" the conventional modes of the novel form in order to express a consistent and meaningful view of the world. His writing is extremely subtle; it reveals many shades of meaning. One does become tempted to find in them scapegoats, victims, Christian symbols, and Catholic masses—some of them blasphemous. If Burgess uses words as a poet does, interpretations of these words are inevitable. But, remembering Burgess's advice to critics in "Dear Mr. Shame's Voice" (published originally in *The Spectator* and reprinted in *Atlas*) about the Joyce "industry" so diligently grinding away in American colleges and universities, one steps diffidently through the pages of the novels. Burgess's novels are indeed entertaining, but, more importantly, they reveal ever deepening shades of meaning as they are reread, meanings that challenge the imagination as they force the reader to consider the human plight.

CHAPTER 2

Themes, Patterns, and Directions

SINCE 1956, when Burgess published *Time for a Tiger,* his reputation has steadily improved in the world of serious literature; today, he ranks in the forefront of those writers who regard the novel as one of the highest fulfillments of art. Each of Burgess's novels since *Time for a Tiger* has demonstrated a growing awareness of what the novel can be made to yield; each novel has been in one way or another an experiment with form or technique or both; and each novel has demonstrated a full appreciation of the limits to which the novel can be pushed before ceasing to be a novel and becoming something else.

One of the first things that the critic becomes aware of is Burgess's prodigious versatility as he attempts, first, to define the various "kinds" of novels that he as author is creating, and, second, to submit that "type" to a singular concept, plan, or variation. Although Burgess experiments constantly, his novels are not simply exercises in form or technique, although they may appear to be little more than that to his reviewers. Careful examination of his techniques and of his thematic development reveals that Burgess's ultimate concern is to communicate his ideas within the traditional forms of the novel while, at the same time, testing the strengths and limitations of that genre. The fact that he is the funniest writer of serious satire since Evelyn Waugh frequently sidetracks his reader; for, on occasion, Burgess's comedy is so hard-hitting or so punch-happy that it prevents a sympathetic appraisal.

I *The Craftsman*

Burgess has written in *The Novel Now* that he regards his books as works of craftsmanship, just as a carpenter so regards the chair that he makes; but the facts reveal that he is much more than a commercial entertainer. Indeed, as he himself points out, the writer has to put bottom to chair and pen to paper to earn a living; but *how* the pen is put to paper and *why* reveal the difference between an artist and an artisan. In *The Novel Now*, Burgess says of himself and his methods: "Critics have said that there are certain persistent themes in my novels—the need to laugh in the face of a desperate future; questions of loyalty; the relationship between countries and between races. I am not qualified to discuss my works in terms of subject-matter; I have enough to do in trying to write well, which is not easy: the writer concentrates on his craft, the critic looks over his shoulder at his art, such as it is."[1]

Burgess's other comments as a critic about the novel form as it has been employed by writers since World War II reveal Burgess the artist's preoccupation with structure, theme, and technique. In the December 4, 1966, *New York Times Book Review*, Burgess humorously suggests that the Chinese Taoist concern for yin and yang can be applied to the novel: "The Chinese Taoists posit (if Comrade Mao still permits) a universe in which the yin (or female principle) battles endlessly with the yang (or male principle). There is even a Chinese disease, sometimes fatal, in which the male believes he is being set upon by the yin, so that the emblems of his sex shrink fearfully into his belly. I think I suffer from this disease."[2] Needless to say, Burgess, his comments notwithstanding, gives evidence of thoroughgoing yang; for his works are, in the final analysis, robust, forceful, Rabelaisian, darkly Swiftian. His novels show a wide reading and an acute appreciation of the best aspects of English and European literature; for, even though he writes about Malaya and sets his pieces in Brunei and in Russia, he belongs within an English tradition. Besides those mentioned above, the chief influences on his writing are Henry Fielding, H. G. Wells, J. B. Priestley, Aldous Huxley, Rudyard Kipling, and Gerard Manley Hopkins—all more yang than yin, it would seem. These writers indeed influence his style and his techniques; but ultimately Burgess assimilates all influences; and his novels become, despite a I-have-been-there-before feeling on the reader's part, unique manifestations of a strikingly inventive talent.

In *The Novel Now*, Burgess asserts that few writers today care sufficiently or believe enough to write masterpieces that "spring out of conviction" (18). Since the majority of contemporary novelists do not feel sufficiently or strongly enough about either the world or, unhappily, about the art of the novel, such great, large-scale, or panoramic novels as Leo Tolstoy's *War and Peace* or Cervantes's *Don Quixote* are no longer possible. Two exceptions, although they are flawed in many ways, are Thomas Mann's *Doctor Faustus* and Boris Pasternak's *Doctor Zhivago*. "Perhaps the times are no longer propitious to the production of masterpieces which both embrace and enhance life," Burgess writes. And, in his assessment of the novel, he approaches the writers he considers in terms of their *oeuvre*. He assesses the novelists emerging since 1939 on their ability to "present fragments of an individual vision in book after book, to build if not a *War and Peace* or *Ulysses*, at least a shelf" (19).

Burgess adds to this discussion of the fragmentary nature of contemporary art in his study of James Joyce, *Re Joyce* (*Here Comes Everybody* in England):

The great novels of the past—*Don Quixote, Tom Jones, War and Peace*, for example—have all been very long, and it is only in great length that novelists can fulfill their blasphemous urge to rival God. To create a few human beings in a segmentary context of life is well enough for a minor artist, but the major artist wants a whole cosmos and the whole of mankind. He cannot really have all this—Joyce, like Blake, was able to achieve it by making one character play many parts—but he can at least create a big human community which is a sort of reduced image of the cosmos.[3]

This last statement is significant in an appreciation of Burgess's contributions to the art of the novel, for he has attempted to create a "big human community which is a sort of reduced image of the cosmos"; indeed, he has achieved much more than a portrayal of the "segmentary context of life," perhaps because, as has been indicated earlier, all of his novels are in some way allegorical, because they are all in some way religious, and because they are all in some way filled with the adventure of achievement and of failure. The facts reveal, indeed, that Anthony Burgess is not a "minor" artist but that he is one of the most significant, important, and dazzling writers to come upon the literary scene since Graham Greene stopped shocking and settled down to being philosophical. Perhaps the fact that Burgess submitted himself to the discipline of musical composition exempted him from the usual adolescence of most novelists; for, from *Time for a Tiger* until the appearance of *Enderby*

Outside, the reader is forced to admit to writing of the highest quality. There is nothing slapdash or amateurish about Burgess's work. He dazzles, bewilders, teases, beguiles; but, best of all, he succeeds.

II *Levels of Meaning*

Burgess's method, overall, in his novels is allegorical, yet his individual pieces are by no means point-for-point allegories, as is William Langland's *Piers Plowman,* John Bunyan's *Pilgrim's Progress,* or even Graham Greene's *Brighton Rock.* His method, as he himself has said, is that of life itself; for all of man's actions and words are no more than signs or symbols, tremors of his intentions. The essential meaning is almost always the hidden one. Rex Warner, an allegorist of superb skill, defines the allegorical method as follows: "Most people's minds seem to turn away with a kind of distaste from the notion of allegory. And yet a great part of their speech and action, most of their jokes, much of their entertainment, their pleasures, their complicated thought, their philosophy are allegorical. Strictly speaking, according to the dictionary, allegory is 'other-speaking,' the describing of one thing under the guise of describing another. A little consideration would show how full our ordinary conversation and ways of thought are of allegory."[4]

Rex Warner admits that allegory and the allegorical method are viewed with suspicion by the Realist critics who insist that, if an author has anything to say, he say it directly. Early allegorists, like John Bunyan and Jonathan Swift, Warner says, expressed their ideas in ostentatious and matter-of-fact ways. Dickens and Dostoevski indulged in dreams and nightmares, visions, monstrosities, madness. They seemed to say, Warner insists, "Look carefully at these strange creatures we show you. You and your world are like this" (146). Modern allegorists, however, reverse the process: " 'Here is your world,' they say; 'look at it in a slightly different way and you will see how full it is of monstrous and unrecognized forces'" (146). Anthony Burgess, fascinated by words—their denotative meanings as well as their implications—fulfills in his novels the definition of "modern" allegory cited immediately above.

Like James Joyce, Burgess is not only an admirer of language but a student of it. To him, as to Joyce, the use of words, from whatever language they derive or from whatever languages they are concocted, is an action of metaphysical importance, a sacramental action. In *Language Made Plain*, primarily a scientific-linguistic study, Burgess insists over and over again on the power of language: "language survives everything—corruption, misuse, ignorance, ineptitude. Linking man to man in the dark, it brought man out of the dark. It is the human glory which antecedes all others. It merits not only our homage but our constant and intelligent study."[5] And, in his use of words, Burgess is almost as deceptive and whimsical as Joyce, as demanding and insistent as Gerard Manley Hopkins—almost. In all of his novels he manages, indirectly, sometimes capriciously, to reveal his essential meaning. Yet he never forgets the surface story; he entertains as he beguiles, making his reader laugh as he teases him into considerations of moral and ethical import.

Speaking of the art of Franz Kafka in *The Novel Now*, Burgess says: "We have all come to feel a powerful and desperate guilt since the revelations of Belsen and the blasting of Hiroshima: there are few of us now, Christian or not, who would reject the doctrine of Original Sin. And with the breakdown of society as our fathers knew it, the creation instead of huge conurbations where everybody is lonely, the Kafka theme of man's essential isolation strikes at us poignantly. He was the pilot of the pain of contemporary man" (34). Burgess is, as he has written, a Manichaean; but his avowal must be taken charily. Indeed, Manichaeanism is not a pleasant way to view the world, and it undoubtedly appeals to Burgess because it explains to him so much about the condition of mankind, insisting as it does on the duality of nature, man's struggle between the perfection of spirit and the mire of evil. Many of Burgess's major characters are either failed or despondent Catholics; and, like their author, they are fully aware of the "heresy" by which they are tempted.

Still, free will is operative in Burgess's world; and, although Burgess claims to be a Manichaean, he does not insist that his characters subscribe to those theological considerations relevant to the doctrine. Many religious, and even theological, considerations, ideas, and stances, are approached in the novels, but characterization is rarely sacrificed to thesis. Because Burgess deals implicitly, or allegorically, with religious or theological considerations, it would seem absurd to insist upon an Existen-

tialist interpretation of his fictional world, even though such
an interpretation would be entirely possible. He is primarily,
as he insists, a writer of novels, one who deals with philosophical
and religious problems incidentally, one who is concerned with
the fable he is concocting and with the audience to which it
will appeal. In *Books and Bookmen* for July, 1970, he wrote:
"Unfortunately I've had to earn my living writing books—no
priestly vocation like Hopkins, no munificent patroness like the
Harriet Shaw Weaver who helped to support Joyce. This means
that I've had to compromise, avoiding overmuch word play and
verbal oddity, trying to tell a plain story in something like plain
words. But it seems to me that good writing should be aware
of the total possibilities of language and also appreciative of
what language has done throughout the whole period of its
development."[6]

III *Antiheroism and Black Comedy*

Anthony Burgess's first novel, *A Vision of Battlements,* was
written three years after he left his army post in Gibraltar. It
is, when compared to the later novels, an eccentric but none-
theless sophisticated attempt at a mock-epic. Funny, grotesque,
witty, at times pompous, at others profound, the book demonstrates Burgess's ability to deal comically and satirically with
characters and situations. His next novel, that which was published first, called *Malayan Trilogy* in England and *The Long
Day Wanes* in the United States, is set in a Malaya trembling
on its eve of independence. The comic devices that Burgess
used, and learned from, in *A Vision of Battlements* are put to
use in the Malayan novel, and the result is a near-epic. The
protagonist of the novel, Victor Crabbe, demonstrates Burgess's
growth in character development; and, to Burgess, character is
of major importance: "There are certain things that the novel
cannot do without, and the greatest of these is character," he
wrote in *The New York Times Book Review* for August 21, 1966.[7]

In *A Vision of Battlements,* Ennis, the protagonist, shows the
symptoms of contemporary malaise, symptoms which have come
in recent years to describe the anatomy of the antihero. Indeed,
the makeup of the antiheroic personality becomes in Burgess's
novels an important consideration; for he works through many
of the various disguises that the so-called antihero wears as he

confronts a fragmented world. In *The Vision of Tragedy*, Richard
B. Sewell points out that the contemporary antihero struggles
"not so much with a crisis as with a condition; and the condition
is the temporary confusion of values and the dilemma in his
own soul."[8] Beaten down and ignored by society, the antihero
frequently brings about his own destruction and, too often,
that of others.

In the 1930's C. Day Lewis in *A Hope for Poetry* and in the
1940's Rex Warner in *The Cult of Power* pointed out the problem
of the state as antagonist for both the hero and the writer. Both
writers pointed out that the social organism had grown to such
a size that it had complicated man's relationship with the
spiritual life and that man had, consequently, come to associate
his limitations with the state. The potentiality for tragic action,
in either the Aristotelian sense or the Elizabethan one, was
curtailed because the individual could no longer identify an
antagonist as such; the complex and bewildering state simply
defeated him in and by its anonymity. The Aristotelian concept of error in judgment or of the tragic flaw no longer
applying, writers could at best produce domestic tragedies;
Arthur Miller's *Death of a Salesman* and *All My Sons* are two
of the best examples. Graham Greene in at least two novels
struggled with the concept of the hero, and in *The Heart of the
Matter* all but succeeded when he pitted Major Scobie against
a noble antagonist, the God of the Roman Catholic Church. In
The Power and the Glory Greene dealt with the saint, but he
portrayed in striking allegory the power, fascination, and even
the beauty of the power cult in the character of the unnamed
lieutenant. As for the confusion inherent in the concepts of
saint and hero, Martin D'Arcy has observed:

In the Christian scale of values the hero is not distinguished from
the saint; it is more a matter of emphasis than of division. The saint
cannot be canonized unless he is shown to have practiced heroic
virtues; the man of heroic deeds cannot be called a hero unless
there is evidence that his inner spirit corresponds with his deeds,
and that his motives are pure. But whereas in using the word saint,
the emphasis is on man's relation to God and his spiritual work for
his fellow man, it is prowess and self-sacrifice for others, for friends
or a nation, which is uppermost in our thought of the hero.[9]

In Burgess's novels the aspect of sainthood is neither developed
nor overlooked, but it is implied as Burgess constructs the

motivations and moral referents for his characters. In the
Malayan books, Crabbe most approaches the criteria of the conventional hero, but his defeat at the novel's end is more pathetic
than tragic. The antiheroic protagonists, especially Alex of *A
Clockwork Orange,* ironically exemplify a code of conduct by
reacting violently against that which has been thought heroic
by past generations.

In the background of the contemporary antihero lies one of
the most modern heroes of literature, Stendhal's Julien Sorel,
rebel-hero of *The Red and the Black.* One remembers Stendhal's
prophetic words that his art would be recognized fully a century
after his death, the period of World War II. Handsome, brilliant,
Julien Sorel, born a woodcutter's son, storms the châteaux of
aristocratic France. Modelling himself on the defeated Napoleon,
Julien assaults first the gentle Mme. de Renal, but defeats his
intent by falling in love with her. At the novel's end, betrayed
not by Louise de Renal but by the priests who counsel her,
Julien, acting emotionally instead of intellectually, attempts to
kill her. At his tribunal, he turns on his judges and accuses them
of condemning him not for his attempted crime but for his
presumption in rising so high on genius alone. He is convicted
and executed because he has challenged and conquered the
social order. He relinquishes the hypocrisy that he has nurtured
in his combat against society; and he dies, romantically, in the
full knowledge of his victory over his enemy.

In the twentieth century, the antihero is not so lucky as
Julien Sorel, who can identify and scheme against his enemy;
but, like him, the antihero springs from the proletariat. Unlike
Julien, who nurses his hypocrisy warily, the contemporary antihero is loud in his denunciations of social injustice, as blank walls
spring up to obstruct his passage through the streets of belonging.
But unlike Julien, who knows what a monstrous perversion society
is, the contemporary hero is baffled; and he rages as John
Osborne's Jimmy Porter rages in *Look Back in Anger.*
Aware of his lack of opportunity, of his tremendous ego, and of
his will to conquer, he rarely understands the nature of his
rebellion. He feels sorry for himself too often, lacking as he
does the charming cynicism and the self-knowledge with which
Stendhal endowed his protagonist. Like Julien, the contemporary
hero proves himself as he conquers women, borrowing a leaf
from the page of another antiheroic type, the Byronic misan-

thrope. Anthony Burgess's Ennis and, to a lesser degree, his
Crabbe, and his Lydgate in *Devil of a State* fulfill the definition
of the antihero on its simplest and, perhaps, most appealing
levels. But Burgess adds to the portraits of his belligerent protagonists the extra dimension of religious unease.

Although the antiheroic personality figures prominently in
Burgess's shelf of books, it would be ridiculous to suggest that
he is attempting to deal "clinically" with the contemporary
maladjusted individual. All of his protagonists, be they power
addicts or failed romantics, or lapsed Catholics, are aware of
their treachery to some ultimate standard of good; but they
are allowed to develop as they must, exciting the reader as they
move through their antic hays, forcing considerations of moral
and ethical value. Burgess himself defines, briefly, what he
thinks the term "antihero" means in *The Novel Now* when he
writes of Jim Dixon, Kingsley Amis's protagonist in *Lucky Jim*:
"Dixon asks little from life—enough money for beer and cigarettes, a nice undemanding girl-friend—but society has so organized things that he cannot have even this little. What he can
have, what is in fact imposed upon him, is the great post-war
sense of social purpose, hypocritical slogans about education,
culture, progress. . . . [H]e is handed the stone of spurious
idealism" (141).

Burgess further points out that rebels in contemporary British
fiction, instead of going all the way as Julien Sorel does in
The Red and the Black, have a fling before settling down.
Joe Lampton in John Braine's *Room at the Top*, as well as Jim
Dixon, marries above himself—"hypergamy," to use Burgess's
word—desiring to conquer, as Julian had before them, women
above their stations: "This is an aspect of the perennial class
motif that bedevils British fiction," writes Burgess in *The Novel
Now* (141). And he further points out that, although the reader
is meant to sympathize with the antiheroic protagonist, he is
still meant to laugh at him. And this statement introduces the
problem of the black-comic convention that Burgess employs
from *The Right to an Answer* in 1960 to the publication of
Enderby Outside a decade later. Burgess's willingness to employ
the black-comic motifs may, perhaps, be explained by the
answer he gave Lewis Nichols in *The New York Times Book
Review* for April 10, 1966. When Nichols asked him about the
kinds of novels he had written, Burgess explained that he

believes "in the tradition growing up in England to develop the novel in popular forms."[10] And in a review of Mordecai Richler's *Cocksure*, written for *Life* magazine, Burgess expressed a preference for the black and the horrible: "We are conducted so rapidly through the contemporary sewers that the trip seems positively bracing."[11]

As exploited by such practioners of the black-comic "art" as Joseph Heller in *Catch 22*, Terry Southern in *Candy*, and, to a degree, Vladimir Nabokov in *Lolita*, black comedy indicates to many of its admirers and students alike a switch in comic emphasis rather than a new direction in the development of an original form of comedy. Perhaps what best describes and most distinguishes black humor is the strange combination of surrealism and horror that serves it, for the activities described in these novels, as well as in others of the "type," excite the reader as he might be excited by a nightmare; for the emphasis is on logical illogicality as the plot capitalizes on scenes of fear and terror; and it often does so by means of incremental repetition. In other words, the same situation is repeated; and, even though the reader is aware of the repetitions, he is beguiled by them. The constant appearances of Nately's whore in Heller's *Catch 22* serve as an example of this point. Although black humor succeeds in shocking or revolting the reader into some physical response such as horror, terror, or nausea, laughter of a curiously guilty nature results, eliciting as it does so a catharsis of sorts. Indeed, upon reflection, there seems to be little that is new or startling in the manifestations of this "new" approach to comedy, for aspects of black humor can be found in Juvenal, in Jonathan Swift, in Franz Kafka, in Evelyn Waugh, with all of whom Burgess is familiar.

Furthermore, black humorists appear to be dedicated to that which all of the best satirists are dedicated to: the improvement of a social situation, or the correction of a social injustice. Black humorists most enjoy castigating institutions and beliefs generally accepted as "sacred." The more sacred the cow, the greater the abuse heaped upon it. Therefore, institutions and beliefs cherished and even held "sacrosanct" become the fairest game. Laughter results as the reader is first terrified and then made aware of the fact that the institutions and beliefs he has taken for granted no longer afford comfort, that these institutions and beliefs have been turned into monstrous perversions of what

they once meant. Religion, the family, government, war—all
are suitable targets for the black humorist as they have been
suitable targets for satirists since the beginning of civilization.
Laughter results from the juxtaposition of the serious and the
grotesque as emphasis is placed on the macabre and the absurd.
Horror is demonstrated as logically true and as inevitably
probable. The intellectual purport of the scene becomes, because
of the technique of the humorist, a difficult consideration. Guilty
laughter fills the gap between a physical response of revulsion
and the moment of intellectual awareness.

Although black humor such as Heller's and Burgess's relies
on the zany, on slapstick, and on cruelty, it does not differ
substantially from that of Swift, Kafka, Waugh, and many other
writers. Swift's black humor permeates every sentence of "A
Modest Proposal"; the full comic effect is achieved only at the
end when the proposer admits that his wife is past childbirth
and that none of the conditions described in his essay apply
to him. Kafka's Gregor Samsa in "The Metamorphosis" is the
victim of a grim joke, but the humor of Gregor's change into
a cockroach persists, unlike Swift's joke, well past the point
of comic return. In Evelyn Waugh's *Decline and Fall,* white
slavery is made excruciatingly funny through the innocent Paul
Pennyfeather's reaction to it; and the progress of little Lord
Tangent's wound, the result of an accident during school games,
becomes a unifying device paralleling the various stages of
decadence and insanity that the novel confronts.

Anthony Burgess's novels, then, very frequently combine the
antiheroic personality and the devices of the black comedians;
but each novel poses its special problems. Ultimately, there
are no categories; for the majority of Burgess's novels are
attempts to control and conquer, even to subvert, various "kinds"
of novels to his intellectualized and individualized purpose.
Being an artist means for Burgess the mastery of every aspect
of his craft; mock-epic, antiheroism, black comedy, romanticized
biography, thriller—each of these aspects is to be attempted,
to be interpreted, to be tested, to be submitted to the over-
whelming compulsion of the artist to impress his own personality
upon it.

CHAPTER 3

Toward Malaya

"WHEN I first began to write fiction it was, as with most novelists, a refined hobby that, as I got deeper into it, began to demand more time and application than was right for a hobby: it began to wish to be a full time job," writes Burgess in *The Novel Now*.[1] *A Vision of Battlements,* his first novel, written in 1949, three years after he had left Gibraltar, where he had spent three years, was not published until 1965. "The typescript," writes Burgess in the Introduction, "travelled to Malaya and Borneo with me, then back to England, always pushed into drawers but—so loath is the artist to waste anything —never actually condemned to destruction." Sixteen years after the composition of the novel, he continues, he found it possible to read the work with "not as much artistic depression as I might be expected to feel."[2]

I A Vision of Battlements

Richard Ennis, the protagonist of the novel, means a good deal to Burgess "because he is a failed composer" and also because he represents the antiheroic. "In point of public appearance, he limps after the well-known and established rebels; in point of creation he comes pretty early" (8-9). *A Vision of Battlements* is *the* novel, one publisher's blurb lays claim, that introduces the "first" of the antiheroes, thus antedating Kingsley Amis's *Lucky Jim.*[3] Of course, one is reminded of Conrad's antiheroic protagonists as well as of those of Graham Greene, notably Raven who appears in *A Gun for Sale* (1936) and Pinkie Brown of *Brighton Rock* (1938). Still, Burgess's hero is a remarkable invention not so much because he appears so early among contemporary antiheroic protagonists but because he looks at the antics of the world from a peculiar perspective which can, for lack of a better descriptive term, be called "comic-black." What is even more remarkable is the fact that

Burgess is among the very first novelists to satirize World War II. For *A Vision of Battlements* was written three years before Evelyn Waugh's *Men at Arms* and six years before Joseph Heller's *Catch 22*, with both of which it has much in common.

That there is, perhaps, more of the passionate Byronic rebel about Burgess's Ennis and less of the pursuer of self-interest or evil that characterizes many later antiheroes enhances rather than detracts from the characterization, even though it denies, to an extent, the claim of originality. Ennis's goodness of heart, his passionate devotion to beauty, and hence to truth, his love of music, and his awareness of good and evil, conditioned by his Roman Catholicism, make him an infinitely more believable and complex character than many more typical antiheroes. Considering the various stupidities performed in the name of duty and common sense, Ennis's actions, rebellious though they are, become, inevitably, devices necessary for him to maintain sanity and balance in a mad and ignoble world. Ennis's excesses are not only comically remarkable, but they are logical and, paradoxically, even admirable; for they bespeak both the passion and ardor of the man. They make the reader laugh as they make him shudder.

Needless to say, *A Vision of Battlements* is a remarkable first novel, a feat perhaps not paralleled since the appearance of Graham Greene's first novel, *The Man Within* in 1929 with which *A Vision of Battlements* has superficial similarities. Both novels make use of the antiheroic protagonist, both deal with the divided personality, and both are concerned with responsibility and commitment. And each novel sounds out and approaches themes that are developed and later exploited. Indeed, like the first chapter of James Joyce's *Portrait*, Burgess's first novel contains, in synoptic form, the entire pattern of his artistic development.

A Vision of Battlements, a mock-heroic treatment of the final months of World War II, loosely follows the action of Virgil's *Aeneid* and was written, partly, to place the author's stay in Gibraltar while in the army in perspective. Of the framework of the novel, Burgess writes:

"Ennis," who tries to blue-print a Utopia in his lectures and create actual cities in his music, is close to "Aeneas," "Agate" to "Achates," "Turner" to "Turnus." Lavinia is Lavinia, Barasi is Iarbas, his name anagramatised. Concepcion is Dido, a dark-skinned widow loved and abandoned. The use of an epic framework, diminished and made comic, was not mere pedantic wantonness, nor was it solely a little tribute to James Joyce; it was a tyro's method of giving his story a backbone; it was also a device—failed, alas—for taming the Rock by enclosing it in myth, which is bigger than any chunk of strategic geology. (8)

A member of the Army Vocational and Cultural Corps (the *Arma Virumque Cano* Corps), Richard Ennis, composer, soldier in spite of himself, is shown in a brief Prologue as being transported to Gibraltar to begin the second phase of his army service. "Dunkirk, . . . and then Crete. They wouldn't let me carry on in a combatant outfit," he tells a very pink Wren (Women's Royal Naval Service) with a Roman nose and tiny teeth (11). His wife Laurel in England behind him, "their love . . . a Troy that a ten-thousand year siege could not shatter," Ennis thinks of Troilus and Cressida and wonders whether love is more important than the urge to build cities (16). "Ocean, be calm! Storm-winds, do not affight!" intones the pink Wren/ muse who is to play the part of the goddess in the ship's concert, "Aoelus, we require a steady stage, / So shut your mouth and cool your senseless rage—" (13). Waving to Ennis as he moves into the future, the blonde Wren goes on to Crete, where Venus was born.

The action of the novel proper begins in Gibraltar twelve months later, *in medias res*, with Ennis protesting his love to the dark-skinned widow, Concepcion. He carries a letter from his wife Laurel in his pocket telling him that she thinks it will be sensible for the two of them to separate. Soon Concepcion tells Ennis that she is pregnant with his child, that she will marry her suitor Barasi; and that she and Ennis must part. Laurel soon changes her mind about a divorce and encourages Ennis to try for a permanent post on Gibraltar so that she can join him there. Ennis suffers a "sea-change": while drunk, he falls into the slimy harbor, accomplishing a portion of his trip to the underworld. He tries to do what Laurel asks about a post, but his attempts to ingratiate himself with Major Muir first, the effete Mr. Withers later, and finally Mr. Bradshaw of the Education Service do not work out. His only solace is composing music, specifically a funereal wedding march for Concepcion and a Passacaglia and Fugue that he works on throughout the narrative. His friend Agate, a ballet dancer who

does exquisite embroidery in his spare time and who represents
the artistic aspects of Ennis's psyche, encourages and supports
him.

With "Yellow hair, straight slimness, wide mouth," Lavinia
appears as Ennis watches the apes lasciviously cavorting in their
cages on the summit of the Rock; to Ennis, however, she is
Laurel/Lavinia, and he cannot rid himself of the double illusion.
He pursues her, as she in her way pursues Turner, tall, muscular,
insensitive. Lavinia, who taunts Ennis with his insufficiency as
a man and with his inadequacy as a musician, betrays him for
Turner. Concepcion dies in childbirth; Ennis inadvertently
causes Turner's death; and Laurel abandons him. The war over,
Ennis, ironically promoted to sergeant major and no longer
sure of his musicianship—his score of the Passacaglia and Fugue
has been returned to him by the British Broadcasting Company
—turns again to England, once more in the company of the pink
Wren with the little teeth and the Roman nose.

In bare outline, Burgess's plot is Virgil's scheme of the
Aeneid; but what lends the novel its distinction and its charm
is the characterization of the protagonist as Burgess involves
him with the army and with the imbecilities that it concocts.
"Arms and the man" is Virgil's theme; "arms and the man" is
the theme that gives Burgess's mock-epic its uniqueness and
originality. Ennis's music, esthetically associated with his Roman
Catholicism, becomes his standard; and he waves it bravely
as he challenges the capricious deity, Major Muir. Proud in his
vision of a city built of art and music, "a universe of ultimate
meaning," Ennis is afflicted by hubris (119). Brought low by
Major Muir's order that he meet three classes in elementary
shorthand on the evening that he is to conduct the concert
that he and Agate have dedicated all their energies to, Ennis
is sacrificed to the cause of army discipline. *"Domine, non sum
dignus,"* he mutters to himself, "as in the past, when the ciborium
had come to him, he had declared his house unfit for the divine
visitant" (119).

Through Major Muir, the deity within the mock-heroic, the
satirical thrusts against the army are achieved: "He had delu-
sions of grandeur and had invented many fantasies about himself
—the many books he had written, the many universities he had
attended. He spoke often ungrammatically, with a home-made
accent in which Cockney diphthongs stuck out stiffly, like

bristles. His ignorance was a wonder. But he had power, pull, in high places, nobody knew how. He was twisted in body, perpetual pain burning out of deep-set rather beautiful brown eyes" (27). The fact that Muir makes it impossible for him to conduct his concert amounts to an "eternal stalemate" in Ennis's view—the constant battle is between good and evil; and the victory seems to be, more often than not, that of evil over good, stupidity over sense. Since his lapse from the discipline of the Catholic Church, Ennis half believes himself to be a Manichee, and as such to be involved in the constant surge of evil's polluted spring. For original sin makes it impossible for man to rise above the inheritance of his evil nature.

The antiheroism of Ennis, then, can be explained on such religious grounds. His failure in love, in education, in art, simply testify to his understanding of the human condition. The concept of the gangster-God replaces for Ennis the concept of the God of love and forgiveness. Although, after his "sea-change" (when he falls into the slimy harbor), Ennis attempts to establish a semblance of order out of the chaos of army life, first by rejecting the filth and squalor that he lives in with his despicable roommate Bayley, and then by joining Agate, he knows secretly that he will fail. The word "hubris" passes through his mind, but he refers his failure ultimately to the evil that is endemic in man since the fall from grace. These points, however, are not insisted upon; they are simply stated. Yet they do go far in explaining the urge that induces Ennis to pay a little native boy "penniques" to deface with the foulest graffiti possible the billets of his superiors who, ironically enough, appear to merit Ennis's vindictiveness. What Ennis actually accomplishes in this act is to smear the face of creation with his disgust of self.

Ennis, however, veers radically from disgust of self to pride in his ability to create beauty. His superior Appleyard says: "Lapsed Catholics are the most dangerous of all religious types. You all become very stoical. Nero had his Seneca, remember. God suddenly leaps out at you and you're not trained to wrestle. You think: 'Yes, it is in the pattern of things to submit, but within, somewhere hidden along the grey corridors, is the real me, the quintessential self, which the evil deity can't touch'" (125). Ennis cannot deny God intellectually. If the filthy Bayley, who sacrifices obscenely to the goddess of Love, represents the bestiality of human nature, it is the effete embroidery-stitching,

former ballet dancer Agate who exemplifies the order and discipline necessary to elicit meaning out of the chaos of human
activity. If Bayley suggests the nausea that he feels for his
physical self, then Agate represents the pride that Ennis feels
in his ability to write music. To dream the dream is not enough,
however. And the concert becomes Ennis's way of challenging
the gangster-God.

If Manichaeanism keeps reminding men of their sinful origin
and prevents the creation of beauty, then it is its opposite—
Pelagianism—that encourages men to persist in the attempt to
achieve perfection. "You heard of Pelagius?" asks the American
Captain Mendoza of Ennis, "Morgan, his real name was. Greek
and Welsh for 'Old Man of the Sea.' He's been called the great
British heretic. He didn't hold with Original Sin" (167). "I've
heard of him vaguely," answers Ennis, as Mendoza, a student
of history, continues: "He was the father of the two big modern
heresies—material progress as a sacred goal; the State as God
Almighty. . . . One has produced Americanism, which is only
a mental climate. America's not real, it's an idea, a way of looking
at things. And then there's Russia, the end product of the
Socialist process. We're both the same, in a way. We both offer
supra-regional goods—the icebox and the Chevrolet or the
worker, standardized into an overalled abstraction at a standardized production belt" (168).

Muir represents, however, within the mock-heroic structure
of the novel, the capricious deity. When he returns to England
to receive his colonelship, where he incidentally meets Ennis's
wife Laurel, the men of his command, encouraged by Captain
Appleyard, decorate the walls of their classrooms. Ennis creates
several murallike decorations in one of which Muir, in the
shape of an octopus, crowns the summit of the Rock. Appleyard is dubious about the fresco and asks Ennis whether there
is satire involved: "Not at all, sir . . . As you yourself undoubtedly
know, the octopus has always, in the folklore of Southern peoples,
been a father totem. This symbolizes the paternal solicitude which
our Major has for the intellectual welfare of the Garrison" (137).
But Julian Agate's fresco, which is even more remarkable, depicts
in a charming and rococo manner the loves of Zeus: "The god
was depicted as descending on Leda, Danae, Europa. The face of
Muir crowned the body of the swan, the huge frame of the bull,
and glinted through the shower of gold. In each case the copu-

lation was presented in frank detail, but any suggestion of the pornographic (though in strict etymological sense the paintings were all of that) was mitigated by the pennant labels attached to the ladies: Art, Science, Technology" (138). "Rather sweet, don't you think, sir?" asks Julian.

Captain Appleyard, however, orders that the walls be restored to their original, dull whiteness. But the joke is on Ennis: he receives a letter from his wife telling him of her encounter with Muir. Ennis wonders whether it is so terrible to be cuckolded or half horned by a god; probably it is in the nature of things. He writes to Laurel, again protesting his faithful love. Then he attempts to bribe Juanito to "make one hell of a mess" out of Muir's billet. The little Juanito, who refuses, knows perhaps instinctively the ire that a god can visit upon a mortal for violating Olympus (142-143).

Ennis, always popular with his men—primarily because he either dismisses his classes or lets them go early—suddenly finds himself the hero of a popular cause. His vision of battlements, his love of freedom and of beauty, communicates itself to the men. Angry at being kept in subservience to army powers once the war is over, the men stationed on Gibraltar grow restless, band into groups, and begin to agitate for repatriation. The Gibraltans also begin to agitate for freedom and independence. Despite the fact that Ennis tries to speak placatingly to both groups, everything that he says is interpreted wrongly, or perhaps correctly, by them. "Now I'm going to talk about something entirely different," he says at one point to an agitating group, as he attempts to turn the discussion away from topics such as want, squalor, sickness, and God (212). "I see we have a piano here. . . . I'd like to tell you a little about a man called—" —"Beethoven," cheer the men:

"Every body knows at least a few bars of Beethoven. . . . This, for instance." . . . He hammered out the opening theme of the Fifth Symphony. "Victory!" called a gunner. "Victory for the working classes. The upper classes have had their victory, now it's time we had ours." "No, no, no," cried Ennis. He got up from the piano. "That theme," he said, "means nothing. It means itself, no more. The call of the yellowhammer, the hammering of Fate—these are poetic fripperies. To a musician they mean nothing. Beethoven was a musician, not a fabricator of slogans in sound. Music was his life, he cared nothing for politics. He snapped his fingers at the thunder,

he snapped his fingers at Napoleon. He had absolutely no respect
for authority. He was a man who would not cringe to the powerful.
He was independent, fearless, alone, no base crawler—." (212-13)

"Good old sarge!" cheer the men.

In maintaining the autonomy of art and the right of the
artist to freedom, Ennis adds, of course, still another dimension
to his characterization. But the reader is reminded that Lavinia
has caused him to doubt himself and his art. His revenge on
Lavinia is to get Turner drunk without Turner's realizing what
is happening. He succeeds very well, with Agate's help. When
Turner enlists several bullies to help him beat Ennis, Agate
manages to forestall the beating temporarily. Ennis leaps onto
his motorcycle and speeds to the heights of the Rock, his pur-
suers directly behind him. They overtake him. While protecting
himself from one of Turner's punches, Ennis unintentionally
causes his rival's death. "Watch it," says one of Turner's bullies:

But Turner was too late to watch it. He tried to restore his balance.
It was like acrobatic comedy. One of the sergeants thought it *was*
that and laughed. Turner fumbled for a hold, saying, "Sod it." His
hands wildly played a few rhapsodic bars on the piano of the air
between himself and the rockface. Then he did a dance on one leg,
wildly pressing at a sort of sustaining pedal with it. . . . Then he
went over the side howling, his body bumping against rock, brushing
sparse grass, dryly harping at dry leafless twigs. He was going
down very fast. His howl grew steadily more distant. Fascinated,
they all peered down. It was a hell of a long way down. They
imagined a final bump somewhere down there among the town
lights. Very far down. (223)

Herein black comedy at its most basic can be discerned.

Because he had capriciously submitted several "erotic" poems
by García Lorca and Saint John of the Cross to be read by school
children during an educational exercise, both Mr. Bradshaw,
who had given Ennis a position in the Education Service, and
Muir, decide that he must go. Ironically, he is promoted to
Warrant Office II. "A crown," says Ennis, "A sacrificial king,"
as Colonel Muir deftly places the insignia of his new rank on
Ennis's arm. "When you get home give my regards to your
wife," retaliates Muir (228).

Before embarking for England, Ennis, reluctantly, because he
is a Catholic and therefore superstitious, submits his future to
Mrs. Carraway, the sybil. Thus an aspect of the visit to the

underworld is accomplished. The Tarot cards reveal a man hanging upside down from a tree, a tower struck by lightning, a bloody moon: "Things have not been going well. . . . Things will not go any better. That's what the cards say. I see birth, but I also see death. I see failure to run a love affair properly. That's in the past" (232). The future for Ennis, Mrs. Carraway continues, offers sacrifice, ruined hopes, somebody's death that Ennis is involved in, though perhaps not responsible for. "It's one of the worst I've ever seen, I'm so sorry," says the sybil (232). She turns then to the crystal ball, which at first reveals nothing; then a priest wearing a robe and carrying a chalice, dipping his hand into the cup and taking out the communion wafer, appears. Beyond that, she sees nothing. When Ennis challenges her to identify the priest, Mrs. Carraway claims that she has not seen his face. Ennis belligerently asks her if the priest's face was his own; but she insists that she does not know.

To test Mrs. Carraway's prophecy, Ennis and Agate leave Gibraltar for Spain to seek information about Concepcion. From Barasi Ennis learns that Concepcion has died in a miscarriage, proving the sybil's clairvoyance. Agate comforts Ennis by reminding him that on the next day he will be leaving Gibraltar for a new world: "Wide boys, drones, a cult of young hooliganism. State art. Free ill-health for all. Lots and lots of forms to fill in. The *Daily Mirror*'s increasing circulation. Nostalgia among ex-flying types, sick for the lost mess games. Returning corporals killing their wives. Bureaucracy growing like a cancer. Reality will seem very unreal over there. . . . A great weight will have been taken off your mind" (261). When Ennis answers that he must learn to grow up, he perhaps means that he must learn to reconcile the division that is in himself.

Considering the period in which the novel was written and the method in which it presents the times, *A Vision of Battlements* is an astonishing first novel. The character of the antiheroic protagonist, as he veers from the baseness of Manichaeanism to the irresponsible freedom of Pelagianism, is indeed a remarkable achievement. This character, who is almost prophetic in his outlines, appears again and again in the novels that follow. He may dress in different clothes and wear a different face; he may confront new and more challenging occasions; at times he may be more sophisticated, at others less aware of the human predicament than Ennis is; but there is something of Ennis in him.

Yet for all of this similarity to other Burgess characters, Ennis succeeds in his own right, just as *A Vision of Battlements* succeeds on its own terms. The novel, comically hinged on the activities of Virgil's epic, makes capital use of the machinery of the epic. One example more perhaps suffices to illustrate this point: the epic games become physical training exercises conducted by Turner and his bullies. But Ennis cannot submit himself to the physical discomfort and psychic bewilderment that the exercises cause him. The scenes describing the bureaucratic and Fascistic arrangements made by the despotic officers in charge of the men afford moments of almost unbearable hilarity. If horror is an aspect of Burgess's art, as indeed it is, then satirical lightness is an equally important aspect of it. The descriptions of the murals celebrating the deity, Major Muir, are also among the funniest passages in the book; for they are realized in terms of the characters and the action as they illustrate the theme of the book. If Burgess borrows episodes and activities from Virgil, it must be remembered that the comic twists and inventions are his own.

But this is by no means to say that the novel is without flaws. The characterization of both Laurel and Lavinia, confused perhaps by the fact that they appear as one person to Ennis, is undeniably weak; and their motivations, especially Lavinia's, are unclear. Concepcion/Dido, on the other hand, although she is briefly sketched, is a remarkable invention; and she emerges forcefully, personifying, even as she emerges, the practicality of Mediterranean peoples, their love of art and beauty and goodness. The reader cannot forget that she and Ennis fell in love while discussing music, that their sin is to both of them similar to that of Paolo and Francesca, and that Dante fainted with emotion when he heard the story of the classical lovers. The introduction of the historic-minded Captain Mendoza to help explain the split in the hero's character seems somehow out of keeping with the general plan of the satire; but again it is perhaps more important at this point in his career that Burgess define, as much for his own benefit as for the reader's, Ennis's nature as he veers from the ecstasy of his musical inspirations to his maniacal desire to befoul the whole world.

Perhaps another unsuccessful aspect of the novel is Burgess's attempt to place the activities of Ennis and Agate in some sort of social perspective. He attempts to do so by introducing

Mendoza as a historian and also by making Ennis himself an
ineffectual history teacher. Burgess does, however, succeed
magnificently in the comic scenes in which Ennis, attempting
to pacify the men, succeeds, instead, in inciting them to greater
manifestations of anger and irritation—he becomes a tool of
historical necessity, perhaps. The mock-heroic exploits of the
hero and the comical sounding of the high-and-mighty theme
through him serve the purpose of perspective adequately. Last
but not least, Burgess demonstrates himself as immediately
aware of and concerned with the problem of living a measured
life in an ordered community. The difficulty of doing so is the
chief problem of his protagonist, and the solution that Burgess
offers Ennis, when Ennis says that it is time for him to grow up,
seems unsatisfactory. Considering the bureaucratic imbecilities
that Ennis confronts, right seems more on his side than on that
of authority; and his immaturity is at least a means of safe-
guarding his sanity.

II Malayan Trilogy: Time for a Tiger

"When I wrote my first novel, *A Vision of Battlements,* I had
no artistic aim other than to recall my wartime life in Gibraltar
and stamp that life, in a suitably depersonalized form, on paper.
I was not even concerned about an audience," writes Burgess
in *The Novel Now.* "But when I wrote my first published books
—the three which make up my *Malayan Trilogy*," he continues,
"I had a strong urge to communicate an image of a Far Eastern
protectorate in a phase of transition" (211-12). Unlike *A Vision
of Battlements,* the *Malayan Trilogy,* called *The Long Day
Wanes* (from Tennyson's "Ulysses") in the United States, was
written primarily for an audience of Malayans but also for one
including everybody else. Burgess, of course, makes no concessions to the reader unacquainted with the historical time
of transition in which the three novels that constitute the trilogy
are set. Malays (opposed to Malayans), Chinese, Indians,
Eurasians, and Europeans move through the activities of the
novel, at first bewildering the reader because of the ethnic
difficulty in which they involve him, then entertaining him by
virtue of their comic brilliance, finally challenging him to a
better understanding of the historical aspects of the novel's
background.

The Malaya that Burgess writes about is, of course, geographically situated in the southern part of the Malay peninsula. Any encyclopedia tells us that it was a member of the British Commonwealth before 1957, approximately the time of the novel, and that Malaya comprises the two former British settlements of Penang and Malacca, as well as nine other formerly protected states. Hinduism, Buddhism, and Christianity are the chief religions of the area; and Dutch, Japanese, Ceylonese, as well as British influences are apparent in the culture.

In 1946 the British established the Malayan Union, taking in all Malaya except Singapore; and in 1948 the union was reorganized as the Federation of Malaya, under the command of a British high commissioner. Political unrest led to war between Malayan guerrillas and British troops. In 1957 the British made further concessions leading to self-rule, and Malaya was admitted the same year to the United Nations; Communist guerrilla warfare was virtually ended the following year. Since the time of Burgess's novel, Malaya has become a part of the Federation of Malaysia (August, 1963). The Malaya that Burgess writes of is, however, much more than a geographical location in the Pacific and Indian oceans of approximately 690 square miles, with a population of 6,278,578. It is a world of men caught up in the inexorable forces of history.

The first novel of the trilogy,[4] entitled *Time for a Tiger*, was published in 1956; the second, *The Enemy in the Blanket*, in 1958; the third volume, *Beds in the East*, in 1959. Each installment of the trilogy can be read as a novel in itself; but the full meaning is revealed only after the three volumes are considered as an entity. Burgess himself describes the plan of the novel in *The Novel Now*:

When I myself began to write my *Malayan Trilogy* . . . , I saw very clearly how a symphonic scheme (the second movement is a scherzo) would enable me to record, each as a very nearly complete entity, the different stages of an Englishman's expatriate love affair with Malaya, as well as the stage of the process which brought Malaya from British protection to independence. A single long novel would not do: there had to be the feel of a very substantial pause between movements which could, at a pinch, be taken as separate and isolated compositions. (94)

The first part of Burgess's *Malayan Trilogy, Time for a Tiger* is set in post-World War II Malaya, a country on the brink of achieving independence. But the Malaya that Burgess describes

in the trilogy is more a region of the sympathetic imagination
than a geographical location, for the novel deals with the challenges of human understanding. The immediate problem that
the novel confronts is Malayan independence and the prepared-
ness of the polyglot nation to assume responsibility and leader-
ship in a chaotic world. Malays, Chinese, Indians, and Eurasians
move through the pages of the book presenting various religious,
economic, and political problems; and each problem is conditioned by ancestry, pride of blood, and religious conviction. The
English—still holding on to the country but reluctant to accept
the consequences and inevitability of their occupation of the
land—exhibit as much naïveté and bewilderment concerning the
political and economic future of the emergent nation as do the
most remote and unenlightened of the various racial and religious
groups that comprise the geographical areas soon to be united.
"The time is coming for them to leave the East," says Mr. Raj
at the end of *Time for a Tiger* of the English establishment.
"At least, the time is coming for those who will not be absorbed.
One cannot fight against the jungle or the sun. To resist is to
invite madness" (173).

Suggestive in a number of ways of E. M. Forster's *A Passage
to India,* Burgess's trilogy, like Forster's novel, transcends its
immediate theme, the formation of a nation, and deals with
human affections. Like Forster's Fielding, Burgess's protagonist
Victor Crabbe is involved in education; and, like Fielding,
Crabbe prefers to remain outside the orbit of the English colony.
After six months in his job as a history teacher in the Mansor
school, he has reached the position of believing that a white
face is an abnormality in a land inhabited by golden-skinned
people. To Crabbe, the ways of the West are eccentric in a
country drenched by the sun, inundated by the rains, and
threatened by the jungle. Yet he recognizes that he is a part
of a historical process that makes his presence in the federation
inevitable:

His being here, in a brown country, sweltering in an alien classroom,
was prefigured and ordained by history. For the end of the Western
pattern was the conquest of time and space. But out of time and
space came point-instants, and out of point-instants came a universe.
So it was right that he stood here now, teaching the East about
the Industrial Revolution. It was right that these boys should bellow
through loud speakers, check bombloads, judge Shakespeare by the

Aristotelian yardstick, hear five-part counterpoint and find it intelligible. (51)

Located in Kuala Hantu, where the Lanchap meets the Sungai River, the Mansor school in which Victor Crabbe works as a history teacher had come into existence as an inevitable consequence of the westernization of the East. Sultan Iblis, a friend to Stamford Raffles, "crashed his mighty fist on the table, slaughtered a few Bugis, tortured a few chiefs, reformed the laws of inheritance," and opened the area to the West (31-32). Following Iblis, Sultan Mansor became an Anglophile, was graciously received by Queen Victoria, "and established that tradition of heavy gambling which has ever since been a feature of the royal house of Lanchap" (32). Fascinated on his first visit to England by the English public school system, Mansor dreamed of an Eton, Harrow, or Rugby in his own country: "He wanted a school for the Malay aristocracy of his own state, but . . . would not but see that his own loins would never produce a sufficient first-form entry in his own lifetime" (33). His successor, Sultan Alladin, saw "in the mingling of many cultures the possibility of a unique and aesthetically valuable pattern, and before his early death he had laid out his plan for a Malayan public school in a letter which he sent to all the Sultans" (34). An able inspector of schools called Pocock next spoke with energy and zeal to the high commissioner who soon saw "the value of an educational establishment which would be a microcosm of the teeming various world which was Malaya and yet be a symbol too of the calm British governmental process" (34).

The school becomes for both Crabbe and the reader a means of understanding and evaluating the various conflicts to be reconciled before the federation can assume the independence that space and time have made inevitable. Chief among the problems confronting an independent country is, understandably enough, that of the Communist ideology. Kuala Hantu is safe enough for Victor to walk around in; but, since it is also a center of Communist influence, its environs are unsafe. In the regions remote from the cities lurk the threats of guerrilla harassments, bombings, and terrorizing. It is not, perhaps, then unlikely that the region geographically called Malaya becomes, in terms of the ultimate meaning of the novel, the world itself. If the school suggests Malaya, then Malaya represents the world.

Thirty-five years old, married to his second wife Fenella, a
blonde and lovely woman superficially interested in art, literature, and anthropology, Victor Crabbe is enslaved by the memory
of his first wife who drowned one icy January day when their
car skidded through a weak bridge fence and plunged them
both into icy waters. Like Graham Greene's Arthur Rowe in
The Ministry of Fear, Crabbe lives a life haunted by guilt, for
he feels that he was in some way responsible for the death of his
wife. So determined is he to remind himself of the event that
he refuses to drive a car. The fact that, unlike most Europeans,
he walks wherever he goes occasions a certain amount of merri-
ment and bewilderment on the part of the natives; yet, paradoxically, it makes him more like them.

Six months in Malaya have already aroused in Crabbe a
genuine love of the people. When Fenella, who is homesick for
England and the ways of Western civilization, urges him to
reconsider his commitment to the Mansor school and to Malaya,
Crabbe reflects: "I should want to go home, like Fenella. I
should be so tired of the shambles here, the obscurantism, the
colour-prejudice, the laziness and ignorance as to desire nothing
better than the headship in a cold stone country school in
England. But I love this country. I feel protective towards it.
Sometimes just as the dawn breaks, I feel that I somehow enclose
it, contain it. I feel that it needs me. . . . I want to live here;
I want to be wanted. Despite the sweat, the fever, the prickly
heat, the mosquitoes, the terrorists, the fools at the bar of the
Club, despite Fenella" (57). So enchanted is Crabbe that he
envies the dark, golden beauty of Mr. Roper, a colleague in the
school who despises himself for his Eurasian background; so
enchanted is Crabbe that his choice of a native mistress, Rahimah, seems but a logical consequence of his romantic attitude.
Strangely enough, however, it is not so much Fenella whom he
feels he betrays with Rahimah as his first wife. The heat of the
South Pacific may, in fact, be a means of staving off the memory
of the icy English water into which he plunged with his wife
eight years before the events of the narrative.

It is Fenella's desire to have a car—she wants to attend some
of the cultural activities that take place in the town near the
school—that brings Nabby Adams and Alladad Khan into Victor
and Fenella's orbit. They are, however, introduced into the
narrative by means of a contrapuntal device that establishes

the inevitability of their meeting. A *bilal* is heard chanting from his minaret, "There is no God but God"; Victor and Fenella, Nabby and Alladad Khan are mystically brought into the pattern of each other's activities. Each awakens to a Malayan morning that announces itself as a state rather than as a process (18). As in *A Vision of Battlements* not only is music used in *Time for a Tiger* as a device to lend unity to the events of the narrative, but also to point out the common aspects of humanity that link the characters to one another.

A contrapuntal device is also used to establish a historical perspective in order that Victor's presence in Malaya can be established as a "time point": Burgess recounts in brief snatches the history of the area while giving the reader necessary information concerning his characters. The greater part of the book, however, deals specifically with Crabbe's psychological validity, with his humanity and his failure, whereby an Aristotelian note is struck, a peripety or reversal; for at the end of *Time for a Tiger* Victor's utility to the people he has grown to love is denied. For the ruse that the schoolboys used to rid themselves of the despotic headmaster Boothby makes instead Crabbe's presence in the Mansor school impossible; Crabbe is blamed by Boothby for the boys' refusal to participate in the school games and dismissed; and Boothby's appointment to another school comes too late for anything to be done. Boothby, who expels a boy for "kissing" on the school grounds, prefers to ignore Crabbe's warning to watch for Communist activities among the older boys. Boothby's morality is Victorian; and he refuses to accept that which he represents, the technology of the West.

Nabby Adams, married to his bottle of warm Tiger beer, which explains the novel's title on one level, always in need of alcohol, in debt to every *kedai* keeper within the area of Kuala Hantu, followed by his affectionate and mangy mongrel dog Cough (whose name is a contraction of an Anglo-Saxon obscenity), is a figure of myth, as Fenella rightly observes when she first sees him. Soon her affection for both Nabby and Alladad Khan causes her to talk less and less about returning to England. Nabby's remarkable expressions begin to appeal to her bookish nature, and she never ceases to be surprised by the quality of his mind and by the range of his knowledge. Perhaps a Eurasian, six feet, eight inches tall, Nabby becomes for Fenella a Prometheus being pecked at by the eagles of debt and drink, a minotaur

howling helplessly in the maze of debt. When she reads to Nabby
and Alladad Khan from Eliot's *The Waste Land,* Adams says:
"He's got that wrong about the pack of cards. . . . There isn't
no card called The Man with Three Staves. The card what he
means is just an ordinary three, like as it may be the three of
clubs" (120). And Alladad Khan in turn nods gravely that he
understands what the thunder says.

What endears Nabby and Alladad Khan to Victor is their
love of the people and their interest in language. And to Burgess
the ability to use the language of the place becomes an effective
means of leading the reader to appreciate and understand the
characters' feeling for and understanding of the people among
whom they live. Alladad Khan, at first interested in Fenella's
blonde womanliness, soon discovers, as he learns English and
she Malay and Urdu, that it is what she represents to him as
a woman of the West that is important to him. Summoned by
the prayer of the *bilal,* Crabbe and Fenella, Alladad Khan and
Nabby Adams, accompanied always by the smelly dog Cough,
explore together the familiar and unfamiliar terrain of human
involvement. Again one is reminded of Forster's method in both
A Passage to India and *Howards End;* in fact, the same sort
of gentle irony and whimsical satire pervades the narrative at
those points when the four are together.

An officer in the motor transport division of the British army,
adept in tinkering with engines, Nabby offers to buy an Abelard
automobile for the Crabbes. He tampers with the engine,
convinces its owner to sell it to him at a low price, restores the
engine, and then sells the car to Victor at a profit, thereby
temporarily relieving the pressure of his own debts. In return
for an occasional use of the car—so he can leisurely journey
into areas remote from the city to drink—Nabby offers to keep
the Abelard in repair. Since Victor will not drive, because of
his accident of eight years before, Adams's corporal Alladad
Khan offers to drive Mrs. Crabbe wherever she wishes to go.
Fenella, who had originally wanted to go to the city to see
"art" films, suddenly finds that she is interested in the "real"
Malaya, thereby reminding the reader in her ingenuousness of
Forster's Adela Quested who had wanted to see the "real" India
and had shrunk fearfully from it when it revealed its presence
to her at the Marabar Caves.

To maintain the automobile and to pay Alladad Khan for

chauffeuring Fenella, Victor is forced to end his relationship
with Rahimah, a fact which sets a comic plot mechanism to
work. To regain Crabbe's affection, Rahimah bribes Ibrahim,
the Crabbes' homosexual servant, to put a love potion in Victor's
drink. Ibrahim, who takes the eight dollars and buys himself
some beautiful sarong material with the money, delays putting
the potion into his *tuan*'s drink until he decides to abandon the
Crabbes for a planter who himself has been abandoned by a fair
young friend in the Drains and Irrigation Department. When
Victor and Fenella drink the potion together—Ibrahim has put
it into a bottle of sherry—they, like Tristan and Isolde, rediscover
each other, all to the accompaniment of the Liebestod. The
important point, however, is that Victor suddenly realizes that
the compassion he has felt for Fenella has, if only temporarily,
turned into a stronger emotion. Rahimah for her part manages
to capture a wealthy and decadent young raja, and the love
potion thus yields a comic double dose.

It is the journey to Gila, a little town on the state border
where Nabby has to go to inspect cars, that dictates the symbolical meaning of the novel. Ostensibly a trip into a picturesque
area of the country suggested by Nabby to repay the Crabbes
for their hospitality, the journey becomes a voyage into the
mysteries of the heart. To reach Gila, the Abelard must travel
through an area of approximately nine miles in which there is
much terrorist activity. The arrival in Gila is delayed first by
the rains, then by Fenella's illness. The rain becomes the travel-
ers' world, for there is no other vehicle on the road: "Perhaps
they had missed the announcement? Perhaps the living and the
newly-risen dead had all been instructed to report at some great
town of stilled factories and parked cars, no more to be used,
for there, at the zenith, in the rain of the Last Day, He stood
in His glory, flanked by seraphic trumpeters. . . . They carried
guilt, like an extra spare-wheel, in the boot" (127).

When the rain ceases Fenella feels ill, but she is reluctant
to ask the party to stop since it is deep in the zone of terror. To
make matters worse, she is forced to support Nabby's shaking,
panting dog on her lap. The landscape that the Abelard traverses
is that of a surrealistic, suffocating inferno: "The road ran
sluggishly between the deep beds of lianas, hacked out of
sweating, breathless, obscene, sunless greenery. The tree-tops
could not be seen. The sky was choked by the tangled limbs

and fingers of parasite growths which choked and sucked their sky-high hosts. There were no noises. Only a snake wormed in front of them, then swam like a fish through the green sea of jungle floor" (128). When the party arrives within sight of the town, Fenella is sick, and the jungle locks its cage. The tiger of the novel's title has sprung. The voyage to Gila brings into prominence the religious importunities of the novel's theme, and the allusion to Blake's poem, "The Tiger," tentative before, suddenly becomes obvious. The inferno imagery, the suggestion that the dog Cough must, like Cerberus, be appeased, the reference to the evil snake gliding through the jungle and to a monkey making a disturbance in the trees—all the surrealistic aspects of the episode support a religious as well as a psychological interpretation, a voyage to the heart of darkness.

Victor, Fenella, and Alladad Khan leave Nabby in Gila and begin the trip back through the jungle. First delays, then a breakdown, and then a Communist-inspired "incident" as the car is entering the city keep Victor from arriving on time at the school games that he is scheduled to supervise. The incident on the outskirts of the city, however, forces him to take the wheel of the car after Alladad Khan is shot. The refusal of the boys to participate in the games is blamed on Victor, who is reprimanded by Boothby and relieved of his post in the school. Preferring to believe a troublemaking boy, "an enemy in the blanket," Boothby ignores both Victor's protestations of innocence and a letter that gives him proof that Victor is innocent of the charge. The voyage to Gila, nevertheless, had brought Victor to a better understanding of himself and Fenella. His intuition, however, had told him that he could have kept the boys in line had he been present during the activities.

Upon his return from Gila, Nabby Adams rather miraculously finds himself the possessor of a winning lottery ticket. Victor, who holds the ticket for Nabby, inflicts a full measure of revenge on Boothby when he shows him the ticket and pretends that the $350,000 prize is his. Nabby, however, does give the Crabbes ten percent of his prize money, enough for them to start a school if and when they return to England. Nabby pays his debts, Alladad Khan is promoted to sergeant and reconciles himself to his wife and his infant daughter, and Victor and Fenella prepare to leave the Mansor school.

The novel ends during the Christmas season, in flood time,

reminding the reader of the Krishna celebrations at the end of
A Passage to India. When Victor asks the gentle Mr. Raj at the
farewell dinner, given by the masters for both himself and
Boothby (who would have been a "decent little school-master"
if he had stayed at home), if his life will be ruined by the East
as Boothby's has been, Mr. Raj replies: "Oh, yes":

But with you it will not be a pity. The country will absorb you
and you will cease to be Victor Crabbe. You will less and less find
it possible to do the work for which you were sent here. You will
lose function and identity. You will be swallowed up and become
another kind of eccentric. You may become a Muslim. You may
forget your English, or at least lose your English accent. You may
end in a *kampong,* no longer a foreigner, an old brownish man with
many wives and children, one of the elders whom the young will
be encouraged to consult on matters of the heart. You will be
ruined. (174)

As Mr. Raj prophesies Victor's assimilation into the luxurious
East, the boys yell, "Crabbe for Head!" To which Mr. Raj
responds, "That cry is your death-warrant. . . . The proletariat
is always wrong" (174).
   Time for a Tiger develops its theme in terms of satire and
comedy, both dependent to a certain degree on an appreciation
of the eccentric and grotesque. The humor, however, unlike that
of *A Vision of Battlements,* is neither savage nor black. Yet the
novel reflects the same awareness of the problems of a sensible
and sensitive human being living in a world threatened by
stupidity, intolerance, and bureaucracy. Burgess places an emphasis on education, and the antics of the schoolboys and the
masters offer him a certain latitude for comic exaggerations.
But the chief distinction of the novel is the characterization,
which is both comically (Nabby Adams and Alladad Khan) and
psychologically (Victor and Fenella) handled. The voyage to
Gila is the novel's high point of interest, and Burgess chooses
the details of the voyage to the interior carefully to delineate
the fears and guilts of the characters.
   Indeed, a casual reference to Ennis (from *A Vision of Battlements*), who leaves behind a book on "The Something-or-Other
of the Unconscious" by D. H. Lawrence, reminds one of Lawrence's attempt to find a solution for the world's problems through
an appreciation of the body and its claims. The reader also

remembers that the "prophetic" Lawrence dreamed of a world in which color of skin would no longer prove a barrier to understanding. By reference and allusion, as well as by symbolic allegory, Burgess enriches and directs his theme, reconciliation. Mr. Raj's prophecy that Victor may be willingly victimized by the East is doubly pointed: there is Nabby returning to Bombay at the novel's end carrying a doctor's certification that he is a confirmed alcoholic and should, therefore, be served intoxicating liquors in any hotel where he requests them; but there is also the embrace that Victor gives Fenella. The Christmas party in which Nabby and Alladad Khan, Victor and Fenella take leave of one another is a challenge to the future. The partaking of food assumes sacramental aspects, reinforcing the subterranean meaning of the novel.

III   The Enemy in the Blanket

The Enemy in the Blanket continues to follow Victor and Fenella Crabbe as they move from the Mansor school in Kuala Hantu to an unnamed one in Negeri Dahaga, where the "medium of instruction was English" (192). It is a land without history, bulbous with mosques, where Islam is powerful and polygamy is practiced; where Siamese Buddhism further complicates an already complicated religious pattern:

It was a land which had been tardy in yielding to the kindly pressure of the British, and Chinese and Indian traders had been slow to follow the promise of peace and cold justice: Malay land, where the Chinese kept to their shops and ate pork in secret. A mere fifty years before, the Siamese had waived, as also with the neighbor states of Kelantan and Tregganu, the *bunga mas*, the rich golden flower of tribute. A British Advisor had come at a time when a gardened Residency and Sikh guards and a coach-and-four had long been a commonplace on the West Coast. (190)

The land is ruled not by a sultan but by an *abang*, who possesses such titles as "Scourge of the Wicked," "Father of a Thousand," and "Friend of the Oppressed."

The British hardly disturb a timeless pattern in a land where the rivers are still the main roads, although a railway train arrives once a week and an airplane lands daily. The signs of westernization in the country are few—a commercial firm established in a poky office, a cinema or two, a few hotels. But the

natives of Dahaga know that these vestiges of Western culture
will soon be absorbed, just as the Siamese had been after the
war, once the Japanese had left the land: "The future would be
like the past—shadow-plays about mythical heroes, bull-fights
and cock-fights, top-spinning and kite-flying, sympathetic magic,
axeing, love-potions, coconuts, rice, the eternal rule of the
Abang" (192).

When the narrative proper begins with the Crabbes en route
to Dahaga, both are troubled by hangovers, the result of a "goodby party" given in their honor in Kuala Hantu. Fenella is as
much troubled by crapula as by an anonymous letter she has
received telling her of Victor's affair with Rahimah. Since no
one meets them at the airport, they engage several trishaws and
attempt to make their way into the city. Their journey is merci-
fully interrupted by Rupert Hardman, whom Victor recognizes
as a schoolmate. Hardman offers them a lift in his car; and a
link with the past is thus established.

Hardman, a lawyer, is imprisoned in Malaya. His income, such
as it is, comes from Malayan clients. Were he to return to
England he could do nothing there to earn a living. His skin
deficient in pigment (he is almost an albino), Hardman had
been in an airplane crash toward the end of the war, and his
face had been burned. Remembering that Crabbe had married a
dark-haired, pretty girl interested in music, Hardman is confused
by Fenella's cool blondeness. He also remembers Crabbe as a
person who had never noticed very much, for the world of
sensory perception meant less to him than the one of theory
and speculation. In his first year at the university, Hardman had
gone to hear Crabbe speak on communism: "Crabbe had had no
interest in the coming revolution, no love for the proletariat, only
an abstract passion for the dialectical process, which he applied
skillfully to everything" (203). Hardman's memory of Crabbe's
intellectual communism becomes later on in the narrative a factor
contributing to Crabbe's second failure in the cause of Malayan
education. It is Crabbe's passion for dialectic reasoning, the
reader learns through Hardman, that has involved him in the
historical processes of synthesis and places him in Malaya.

To meet his creditors and to achieve stability, Hardman plans
to marry 'Che Normah, a good Malay and a good Moslem.
Normah has been married twice before, first to a Dutchman,
then to an Englishman. Both "had wilted under the blasts of

unpredictable passion and her robust sexual demands"; both
had also died suddenly and unpredictably on the eve of their
return to Europe, supposedly at the hands of the Communists
(226). No Cio Cio San, Normah had preferred a wealthy widow-
hood to abandonment in Dahaga. The Communist rifle shots had
simply been Allah's answer to her prayers. To complicate his
relationship with Normah, Hardman is a recent convert to
Roman Catholicism and friendly to Father Laforgue with whom
he occasionally plays chess. According to the marriage contract,
which Normah herself has drawn up, Hardman will renounce
his Catholicism, which means renouncing his friendship with
Laforgue, and embrace Islam. Hardman knows that marriage
to him will cost Normah dearly: an office in town, settlement
of debts, new clothes, a Jaguar. He knows that, although she is
willing to pay, Normah is also determined to get her money's
worth: "There would be invitations to the Residency on the
Queen's Birthday, dances at the club, the prestige of going
about on the arm of a man whose untannable skin could not be
mistaken for that of a Eurasian" (227). In their own way,
Hardman and Normah too are involved in the dialectical process.
At the novel's end she returns to Dahaga from Mecca, carrying
Hardman's child. In attempting to escape from her, to return
to England, Hardman finds death in another fiery crash. The
irony is compounded by the fact that he has been helped in
his attempt to escape Normah and the East by a man with the
same name as the legendary hero of the East—Raffles.

Hardman and Normah are, of course, introduced into the
novel to illustrate facets of the complicated religious and ethnic
patterns that the novel explores. But they are also comic figures
and are infinitely appealing as such. The humor that they introduce into the narrative is doubly effective, aimed at one moment
at the inscrutabilities of the East and at another at the solipsisms
and rationalizations of the West. The Catholic priest, Father
Laforgue, also used for comic as well as for thematic interest,
illustrates the assimilation of one of the West's most autocratic
religions into the ways of the East. Laforgue's meager library
contains works by Confucius and Oriental philosophers, yet
"[n]owhere to be seen was the work of a new slick Thomist,
Maritain, von Hügel, even Augustine or Jerome or Liguori"
(233). Father Laforgue's Catholicism is "equivocal," for his real
love is for the Chinese

Again, as in *Time for a Tiger*, language becomes a means of
indicating the dedication of a character to what he believes
in: "In China [Laforgue] had spoken good Mandarin, and in ten
years this had become his first tongue. Here he found himself
with a parish of Hokkien and Cantonese speakers and a few
English people whose language he could hardly talk. His French,
severed from its sources of nourishment, grown coarse through
lack of use, halted and wavered, searching for the right word
which Mandarin was always ready to supply" (233). As Hardman speaks to Laforgue about his approaching marriage to
Normah and his equivocal commitment to Islam, Laforgue
answers, "It isn't just a question of what you believe but of
what you do" (233).

Physically cut off from Rome, Father Laforgue, ironically,
lives more meaningfully the spirit of Christianity; he draws
closer to the people of the East as he grows away from the West:

The doctor, curing diseases in a savage territory, may well have to
meet the medicine-man half-way and submit to the intoning of
spells and the sticking of talismans between the patient's teeth
before plunging his scalpel into the distempered part. And so Father
Laforgue had been willing to falsify the doctrine of the Trinity in
a polytheistic parish, had learned not to be outraged at meeting
Chinese priests who had married. More and more he had discovered
a sympathy for the charismatic churches against which St. Paul
had fulminated. He had held fast to his main function, primarily a
thaumaturgical one: He could forgive sins, he could turn the bread
and wine into God, he could save a dying child from Limbo. Little
else mattered. (235)

His final reaction to Hardman's marriage to 'Che Normah indicates the extent of Laforgue's capitulation to the East; he feels
less professional concern about Hardman's becoming a Moslem
than he would have felt had Hardman become a Protestant:
"Protestantism is a disreputable younger brother but still of the
family. Whereas Islam is the old enemy" (237-238). Towards
the novel's end, Hardman asks Laforgue to administer the Eucharist to a dying man. As a result, the priest is forced by 'Che
Normah and the other Moslems to leave Dahaga for another
area of Malaya, a part of the federation where there are more
Chinese for him to talk to. Father Laforgue too is involved in
the process of synthesis.

For Victor and Fenella the move from Kuala Hantu to Dahaga,

although Victor is headmaster in the new school, is a move away from the usefulness that they had at first felt in the company of Nabby Adams and Alladad Khan and in the Mansor school. The new school itself is a hodgepodge of misrepresentation and erroneous fact-giving, and Victor finds his task almost hopeless: "One young Tamil teacher had assimilated the sound-system of English so thoroughly to that of his mother-tongue that none of the Chinese and Malay children understood him. Others could not be heard beyond the first two rows. A lot of them were teaching nonsense—Hollywood is the capital of America; Shakespeare lived in the Middle Ages; the Malays founded Singapore; 'without' is a pronoun; the kidneys secrete bile. And a loose fluid arithmetic flourished in the number-melting heat, so that most answers could be marked right" (247).

As Fenella grows more and more restless, Victor suggests to her that she return to England where he will join her at the end of his tour of duty. He knows, however, that he himself will return again and again to Malaya for as long as Malaya will let him. For his place is in Malaya; his duty is to prepare the people to accept those aspects of the West that are not wholly evil—to prepare the Malayans to take over the dangerous Western engine (268). He feels that he is one of the few who appreciates fully the fact that the Romantic age of Raffles is ended: "The whole East was awake, building dams and canals, powerhouses and car factories, forming committees, drawing up constitutions, having selected from the West the few tricks it could understand and use" (322). The liberal dream of Victor's youth, the dream of an intellectually aware and responsible world, is given a new chance in Malaya. When Jaganathan, one of his masters in the school, because of a chance remark made by Hardman at a party, accuses him of being a Communist, Crabbe cries: "Oh, God, man, ... it was wholesome, it was good, it was youth. It was right for us then. We wanted to improve the world. We honestly thought that we loved mankind. Perhaps we did. Oh, we found out that we'd been following a false god, but at the time it seemed the only religion for a man of any feeling or intelligence" (300).

Although Victor resents Jaganathan's misinterpretation of his youthful allegiance to communism, he is relieved to find that Jaganathan has not discovered what is really important and of immediate concern to him in his official capacity as headmaster:

the fact that his Chinese cook Ah Wing has been sending the remains of the kitchen provisions to his daughter's husband, a young Communist terrorist. The official interrogation of the Chinese cook, who has a taste for live mice and black cats, had been a linguistic nightmare: Crabbe, Hardman, and Laforgue had translated from English to French to Chinese and then all the way back again. But neither the priest nor the cook had been able to comprehend the seriousness of the offense against the emergency regulations. Jaganathan's threat, that Crabbe apply for a transfer before his early enthusiasm for communism becomes known, irritates Crabbe. The fact that the past keeps impinging on the present, thwarting his desire to do the best that he can to prepare Malaya for the future, bewilders him. Like the memory of his first wife, which continues to haunt him, his early dreams become the immediate threats of the present: they are the "enemy in the blanket" that will let him neither love nor rest.

When Crabbe returns from Kuala Lumpur where he has gone with Anne Talbot, the unhappy wife of his superior, he discovers that his automobile has been destroyed in a garage fire. He feels that he can now, generously, give the car to the Abang, who has made a formal request to "purchase" it. With the insurance money he will be able to purchase a car that the Abang will not covet. More importantly, however, Crabbe begins to appreciate the simple fact that he must not continue to live in the past, that it will reach out and destroy him, as it has reached out and destroyed the automobile. He feels that his affair with Anne Talbot had been not so much a betrayal of Fenella as of his dead wife and the idealistic past they had shared. The journey to Gila had managed to exorcise some part of the past, at least to the extent that he is now able to drive again. Perhaps his infidelity with Anne Talbot has prepared him to appreciate and understand Fenella, who is the present:

Perhaps there were really two kinds of marriage, both equally valid: the one that was pure inspiration, the poem come unbidden; the one that had to be built, laboriously, with pain and self-abasement, deliberate engineering, sweat and broken nails. He saw his unkindness to Fenella, the demon that urged him on to believe that it was all a mistake, that she, in some way, was the usurper. One could not spend one's life being loyal to the dead. That was romanticism of the worst sort. . . . It was time he cleared the romantic jungle in which he wanted to lurk, acknowledged that life was striving not dreaming, and planted the seeds of a viable relationship between his wife and himself. (322-23)

Fenella apparently accepts Victor's protestations of love and fidelity, but he notices pity in her smile. She asks him to go to the beach with her, to go into the water with her. But he cannot, for the fear of that cold January day of the accident is still with him. As he lies on the sand watching Fenella in the sea, he remarks guiltily that the name he is scrawling in the sand is not hers; he feels that neither the dead woman nor the living one wishes to share him. He hopes that Fenella will be able to accept the fact that the past is not part of him but that he is part of it: "She must accept the minotaur. The Labyrinth had many rooms, enough for a life together—walls to be covered with shelves and pictures, corridors in which the Beast echoed only once in a score of years" (332). When Fenella calls to him, he moves toward her into the sea; but he cannot continue and turns, sobbing, back to the shore. His hope to settle the past proves illusory. "I just had to know," says Fenella; and later she writes: "I'm really sorry for you, Victor. I should have had the sense to see before. You've never really been unfaithful to me, because you never started to be faithful. . . . And now I know what I have to do" (333). Fenella understands that it is unfair to force Victor to continue feeling guilty about two people, that she will have to make a life for herself without him.

The life that Fenella plans to make for herself is with the Abang, who had coveted both her and the Crabbes' Abelard from the first days of their arrival in Dahaga. The Abang feels sorry for Victor, who is doubly to suffer—to be robbed of his car and to be cuckolded too. Realistic about his position in Dahaga, the Abang knows that his days are numbered, just as he knows that his descent from the feces of the sacred bull is a myth begun by some vigorous peasant-ancestor to justify the hold he had secured over some senile sultan. Against the day of his exile, the Abang has hoarded money, jewels, cars, and heirlooms in various parts of the world. The worst that can happen to him is exile in Cannes or Capri, marriage to a film star, and the peculiar glamour that the West accords to dispossessed royalty.

The new politics mystify the Abang. He knows that, in an-

other year, the British will be gone and Malaya will be independent. The new government will substitute one bureaucracy
for another, the only difference being that white faces will no
longer give the orders. A new language will be developed, one
appropriate for government directives but, ironically, one that
the Malay proletariat will no more be able to understand than
the correct English of the British, who will be long gone, their
dream blasted. Most of all, the Abang fears the Communist
hordes whose advance parties already crouch in the jungle:
"They had no dream: their feet were firm on the ground, they
were driven by a deadly logic" (271).

The Abang's chief pride lies in his ability to seduce the women
of the West and in the possession of his fleet of cars. The
Crabbes, whose name he finds difficult to remember—"the Prawns
or Shrimps or whatever their ridiculous fishy name was"—are
severally to furnish his last conquests; and that is probably
symbolic too, he reasons (271). He offers Fenella, toward the
novel's end, a position in his entourage. "He wants me to be a
sort of secretary," she explains to Victor after the attempt to
exorcise the past at the beach has failed. "I think I should be
good at that. It means travelling around. It will be good to see
Europe again. But I haven't decided yet." To which Victor
answers, "You are cold-blooded, aren't you?" "It's all for the
best, you know," she retaliates (334).

After Fenella leaves, Victor becomes ill, perhaps because his
enemy Jaganathan is sticking pins in his effigy and roasting
the doll. Hardman comes to borrow two thousand dollars, the
amount Victor has waiting for him in his insurance agency's
office as payment for the burning of his car while he had been
in Kuala Lumpur. He refuses to lend Hardman the money.
His cook, Ah Wing, returns from the jungle with his son-in-law,
the Communist guerrilla, and thirty other Communists who
have been promised amnesty by the government if they will
surrender. Ah Wing counters Jaganathan's spell and restores
Crabbe to health with a potion made of tiger's liver; Crabbe
informs the authorities of the willingness of the group to give
themselves up, and he becomes a local hero. He thus manages
to defeat Jaganathan's rumors that he is a Communist. Soon
he learns that he, Victor, is to have Talbot's post. The position
of headmaster, however, does not go to Jaganathan, who had
coveted it before Victor ever came upon the scene, but to Abdul

Kadir, a Malay, whose language is a triumph of Anglo-Saxon obscenity. "This state's being Malayanized," says Talbot, "and all the top jobs are going to Malays. The Indians and Chinese are not going to like it, but there it is" (349). A photograph in the *Singapore Bugle* shows Crabbe a group of Chinese terrorists boarding a ship that will take them to their Mecca, "to the land of hard work and drab grey uniform for all and sufficient rations and not much fun, his own undergraduate Utopia" (359). He notices one particular smiling face, and recognizes it as the face of Shiu Hung, the Chinese boy whom he had discovered attempting to organize a cell in Kuala Hantu, the boy he had referred to as "the enemy in the blanket." But the face is also his own youthful face, and the wry smile is very much his own.

Such a summary belies, to a certain extent, what gives the novel its greatest validity, the comedy. Sikhs and Moslems, Malays and Chinese parade through the book, underscoring in hilarious fashion the antic movements of the characters involved in the process of history that Burgess defines and illustrates. And the characters are all comic inventions of considerable merit. Herbert Talbot, who reduces his entire life to food, moves through the activities of the plot, eating, eating; the poems he writes describe his constant hunger. Ah Wing, the Chinese cook, feeds his Communist son-in-law, practices witchcraft and chases a Malay girl to steal her cat. The Abang, perhaps the greatest comic character of his sort to emerge since Evelyn Waugh's Seth of Azania in *Black Mischief,* speaks English with an American accent taught to him by a Japanese who had attended an American university. His idiom is that of Hollywood motion pictures. "You're kind of pretty. Pretty as a picture. I guess they all tell you that," he says to Fenella. "I reckon you and me could get together. We could meet some place and talk. We could have a real long talk and get kind of better acquainted" (261). And Victor Crabbe himself, ever a romantic, is willingly enchanted by the luxurious East which, to him, is not the hot and sweaty box room in his school that he calls an office but the need of the people to be prepared for the coming of the West.

IV Beds in the East

Taking its title from *Antony and Cleopatra,* set a year or two later in time, *Beds in the East,* the third installment of the

Malayan trilogy, continues the career of Victor Crabbe. Still romantic, waiting to hand over to the brown man he is training in the education office, he is as before enchanted by the process of history that he is a part of: "when past and future were equally palpable and, opposing, could produce current" (379). His position, "somewhat of a crepuscular one," permits him to assume the attitude of a benevolent overseer to the people he has grown to love and to whose need he is still dedicated. The immediate time of the novel's activity is the dawn of Malayan independence; and Crabbe has anticipated the time by allowing the man he is training to become in effect the man in authority: "So Crabbe demoted himself to the rank of the Duke in *Measure for Measure*, a god whom all men might touch, wandered round the schools of the town to give funny lessons to children ('the white man always make us laugh, make very happy'). Sometimes he would try to do more spectacular good..." (406). The "more spectacular good" that he is attempting to accomplish involves Robert Loo, a young Chinese musician whom he has encouraged (as Ennis had before him). Although Crabbe knows that Robert's musicianship is beyond challenge, he does have doubts about the nature of the musical training that the boy should receive and, more practically, where the money for that education is to come from. The only judgment he could trust, he knows, is that of his dead wife, whose memory he still cherishes. Again the theme of time made palpable—the past controlling the present and shaping the future—dominates the characterization, and in this novel the theme is carried to a final resolution.

The action proper of *Beds in the East* begins at the airport as Crabbe awaits the return of Robert Loo from Singapore where, on Crabbe's insistence and at his expense, the boy has taken his music to hear it played and to have it judged. An "incident" at the airport brings into relief the hostility that exists among the Jaffna Tamils (who are Hindus) and the Malayans. The incident, furthermore, brings together the characters of importance, underscoring comically the fact "that the component races of this exquisite and impossible country just don't get on" (339).

Syed Omar, a Malayan, has attacked the Jaffna Tamil Manian, at whose going-away party the night before he had railed drunkenly. Syed Omar believes, with reason, that Manian has

jeopardized his position with the police department in order
to replace him with a relative. Manian is being seen off by his
friends Sundralingam, Arumugam, and Vythilingam. Also at
the airport are Rosemary Michael, a Malay schoolteacher, and
Jalil, a Turk, who is constantly propositioning her with "come
eat, come drink, come make jolly time," a refrain that runs
throughout the narrative. Rosemary is biding her time, waiting
for her lover Joe, who is in England. Joe is to send for her,
marry her, and transport her to a world of English respectability.

A creature of rare comic value, Rosemary touches and excites
the characters of the novel and, unwittingly, helps to destroy
Crabbe's dream of usefulness. Her beauty serves to point out
a valuable lesson in esthetics, the kinship of the sublime and
the absurd: "The lack of flaw was a kind of deformity. It was
not possible to say what racial type she exemplified: the eyes,
black, were all East—houris, harems, beds scented with Biblical
spices; nose and lips were pan-Mediterranean. Her body . . . was
that of the Shulamite and Italian film stars. The decolletage,
with its promise of round, brown, infinitely smooth, vertiginous
sensual treasure, was a torment to the blood" (373).

Suffering from an Oriental variant of the Oedipus complex,
Vythilingam, the state veterinary officer, pines for Rosemary.
He wants to marry her in order to punish his mother, who has,
in her own time, betrayed him by marrying an Englishman
named Smith. Having retained her Hindu religion, Vythilingam's
mother is concerned about her son's beliefs and with the fact
that he should marry a girl within his faith with a sizable
dowry as well as with a good religious upbringing. Sundralingam
and Arumugam are also concerned that Vythilingam will marry
Rosemary and disgrace the Jaffna Tamils. "She's of very low
caste," Sundralingam says of Rosemary. "I knew her parents
in Kuala Hantu. She knows I knew them, but she once told
me that she was a Balinese princess. On another occasion she
said she was partly English and partly Spanish. It was her
Spanish blood, she said, that made her get so brown so easily.
In England, she said, she was quite pale" (392). And to these
observations about Rosemary's history, Sundralingam adds that
in Malaya there is too much despising of one's own race and
that this attitude will surely be the trouble with Malaya after
independence from England is final. Parameswaran, a friend of
Sundralingam, adds to this the statement that if Malaya were

left to the Malays, "it wouldn't survive for five minutes" (393).
Without the Malays, Arumugam points out, adding another fillip
to the irony, Malaya might be a good country.

Crabbe, who sees the disparate aspects that constitute a
Malaya capable of synthesis, perhaps through culture, perhaps
through education, is for his part accused by both the Malays
and the Tamils of having lost his taste for women and of having
developed one for Chinese boys.

Robert Loo is to Crabbe the means of adding one small but
meaningful component of national pride to a country that must
develop the best aspects of its historical heritage. "It may be
pure illusion, of course, but the image is there, in his music,"
he says to his friend Cheng Po. "It's a national image. He's
made a genuine synthesis of Malayan elements in his string
quartet, and I think he's made an even better job of it in his
symphony" (399).

To implement his dream of helping Malaya achieve the beginnings of pride in its heritage, Crabbe goes first to Nik Hassan,
the information officer. He tells Nicky of Paderewski, and adds
that Robert Loo's symphony could be played as a gesture of
independence; for it clearly and forcefully states in its musical
idiom that Malaya had thrown off the shackles of an alien
culture and achieved a music of its own. "You've got to have
culture in a civilized country, whether the people want it or
not," Crabbe insists (407). All that Nicky can say is that it's a
pity that Robert is Chinese and not Malay; but he promises
to look into the possibility of Robert's symphony being played
for the independence day celebrations. He suggests that a choral
finale might be a welcome addition; and Crabbe, remembering
Beethoven's *Ninth Symphony*, wonders why not. "And if you
could get the orchestra to stand up at intervals and shout
'Merdeka!' Now that would sell it. That really would make it
political" (408). "You can't do that to a serious piece of music,"
responds Crabbe sadly (408). When Nik Hassan tells him later
that a planter called Wigmore, shot by the Communists, has
left twenty thousand dollars to the state, Crabbe begins to see
the solution to the cost of Robert's musical education in Europe.
The money, more than likely, Nicky says, will go to the sultan
for a new car; for the people are happy when they see their
sultan happy.

Robert Loo spends his days in his father's shop, tending to

the accounts and an occasional customer, but mostly translating the noises, sounds, and colors of Malaya into his music. While he is involved in the composition of a violin concerto, wishing he had more practical experience of the instrument, he looks up to see a crate dumped beside the counter. Soon the contents of the crate are revealed, and a juke box, "APOLLO," stands revealed in all its glittering chrome, "a portent and a god." Robert Loo's father, "like a priest with a host, reverently put into the creature's mouth a ten cent piece" (414). Soon all the "colours of the East and all the languages," all that Robert translates into his music, can no longer be seen or heard over the loud blare. Robert's solo violinist, waiting for her music, her bow at the ready, is puzzled by the delay (412-14).

To find the necessary quiet to continue his composing, Robert takes advantage of Crabbe's offer to use his house. He goes there one evening, having left his father, having decided to take advantage of Crabbe's offer to help him get to Europe where he will be able to continue his study. He finds not Crabbe but Rosemary, a Rosemary in tears, who has been betrayed by her Joe for an English girl. Rosemary suddenly becomes a new inspiration to Robert. Without Crabbe to counsel him, he concludes that all the music he has composed is meaningless, that he must now begin to write music that will celebrate the sensual beauty that he has discovered in and through Rosemary. He returns to his family, aware of a new power; but somehow the muse that had before obsessed him, demanding that he compose, and compose again, no longer does so. He destroys his music—all that Crabbe had put his faith into.

The trip that Crabbe makes to investigate the murder of the headmaster of the Durian estate school becomes within the symbolical framework of the novel a recapitulation of the diverse themes that were touched upon, expanded, but left incomplete in the previous volumes of the trilogy. On the train that takes him on the first stage of his journey to the mouth of the river where the estate is located, Victor finds in a magazine a poem written by his wife, Fenella. Certain of the poem's lines suggest a grinning death's-head, and Victor wonders about Fenella and the life she lives without him. Next he encounters Tommy Jones, who sells Malay beer; Jones of course reminds Victor of Nabby Adams and of the trip to Gila, after which he had found himself able to drive again and temporarily close

to Fenella. But the understanding achieved by the trip had
proved meaningful only for a brief time, he remembers. In
Dahaga, Victor had later become involved with Anne Talbot,
Fenella had left him, and again an attempt to bring an understanding of the ways of the West to the East had failed. The
river's water reminds him of the rain that he and Fenella had
encountered on their way to Gila, as well as of the water in
which his first wife had died. Rather coincidentally, Tommy
Jones speaks of Nabby Adams, who could not abide cold beer.

Soon Victor encounters Moneypenny, an assistant protector
of aborigines gone mad; Moneypenny suggests Victor himself.
Although he is not fully aware of the relationship, Victor fears
to be too long in Moneypenny's obsessed company. Through
Moneypenny, he meets Temple Haynes, an American "linguis-
tician" who is attempting by isolating the phonemes to establish
an alphabet without bothering to learn the language. The
British, Victor cynically decides, had been merely gifted ama-
teurs compared to the professional Americans. Temple Haynes
remarks Crabbe's name and mentions Fenella, whom he had
met in London during an orientation he had attended before
leaving for Malaya. Victor wonders again about the coincidence
that has brought him close to Fenella; and suddenly he is
afraid: "It was as though the river and the jungle together were
singling him out for attention, approaching him in terms of his
own past. Death? Did this mean that he was going to die?"
(492). He rejects the idea of death because his useful dream
is still strong within him. But then he remembers again Mr.
Raj, the schoolmaster at Kuala Hantu, who had prophesied
that he never would leave Malaya, just as Moneypenny will
never leave.

Crabbe and Temple Haynes decide to drive to a village several
miles distant to watch a native ceremony, one much like a
shadow play and Hindu in origin, again reminding the
reader of Mr. Raj's prophecy in *Time for a Tiger*. They remove
their shoes. When Victor later puts his on, he is bitten by a
scorpion. Given penicillin by a local doctor, Victor manages
to walk with a cane. Before taking his leave of Haynes, he
secures the American's promise that he will write about Robert
Loo's music to his colleagues who are interested in fostering
the cause of native art. When Victor embarks upon the ship
that will take him to the head of the river, he is somewhat sur-

prised to find himself in the company of Vythilingam, who has left the city to avoid a mother lately arrived with a suitably dowered young orphan for him to marry. The jungle encroaches, the past encroaches too: "There was nothing to believe in except the jungle. That was home, that was reality. Crabbe gazed in a kind of horror mixed with peace at the endless vista of soaring trunks, lianas, garish flowers. They were chugging towards the *hulu,* the head or fount of everything, where there was no pretence or deception" (516). The agony in Victor's foot suddenly brings him to a sharp awareness of his reluctance to live in the present. In the northern dialect of his childhood he says, disarmed by the pain, to Vythilingam and the Chinese assistant manager he is with, "We've got to throw up the past, otherwise we can't live in the present" (517). At the *hulu,* the head of the river, the two halves of the jungle join to become one; the past and the present come together: "The jungle called 'OM,' like the shadow-play, one and indivisible, ultimate numen" (518). The mystical notes suggested in the earlier novels are brought to a crisis.

At the estate Victor meets Costard, a replacement for Coombes, the man he has come so far to see. It soon becomes obvious to Victor that Costard represents all that he, Victor, has been trying to overcome by means of dedication, humanity, and love. "I'm in this game to keep something alive that's very, very beautiful," says Costard: "The feudal tradition, the enlightened patriarchal principle. You people have been throwing it all away, educating them to revolt against us. They won't be happy, any of them. It's only on the estates now that the old ideas can be preserved. I'm the father of these people. They can look up to me, bring me their troubles, let me participate in their joys" (526). Costard and Victor begin to drink the beer that is brought to them at twenty-minute intervals. They listen to records placed arbitrarily on the turntable by the Tamil servant: Beethoven's *Ninth Symphony,* Dame Clara Butt singing "Land of Hope and Glory," and then a Poulenc-like theme that Crabbe listens to at first absently, then incredulously. "Where did you get that?" he asks Costard, "You bloody thief, you stole it" (527). Costard reveals that Victor's first wife had given him the recording, a single impression; that he and Victor's wife had been planning to go away together. Victor insists that such a thing could not be. "I've suffered enough. Christ, I've suffered enough,"

ANTHONY BURGESS

he cries (528). After he leaves Costard, he walks clumsily
to the river to the waiting launch. Vythilingam watches him
indifferently. Crabbe falls into the river and finds the watery
death that he had evaded ten years before. The voyage into the
heart of darkness is completed.

Independence comes to Malaya. Rosemary and Jalil go to
Kuala Lumpur to witness the celebrations. Robert Loo's music,
a pastiche, "film-piano-concerto stuff," listened to patiently by
Temple Haynes's American colleagues, proves unsatisfactory.
Haynes later receives a letter: "What we want is the indigenous
stuff—folk-song and dance, six-tone scales and the rest of it. . . .
This Chinese boy has sort of rejected the native stuff (for
instance, there's not a trace of the Chinese pentatonic in his
work) and turns out very competent imitations of imitations—
second-rate cinematic romantic stuff, complete with big Rach-
maninoff tunes on the violins and chords banging out on the
solo piano" (550). Syed Omar has, however, secured a good
job delivering a newspaper called *The Voice of America*. The
Americans have rented, significantly, the former British residency
as their headquarters. Vythilingam returns to nurse Rosemary's
cats back to health. Temple Haynes cures a speech defect in
Arumugam; Syed Omar's son Hassan, whom Victor had befriended, makes friends with English Teddies, ironically "starting
a sodality that was to prove more fruitful in promoting inter-
racial harmony than any of Crabbe's vague dreams" (547).
Victor Crabbe is written off, swallowed in the process of history,
while Rosemary happily dances at the club.

V Assessment

It is not difficult to express admiration for Anthony Burgess's
Malayan Trilogy. Daringly conceived and brilliantly executed,
the trilogy accomplishes one of the highest aims of art: the
creation of a world complete and entire—and one governed and
controlled by the artist's concept of what is appropriate, true,
and meaningful. As a record of an historical time, the *Malayan
Trilogy* attempts in part to accomplish for Malaya what Conrad
accomplished for Sulaco in *Nostromo*, Stendhal for France in
The Red and the Black, Manzoni for Italy in *The Betrothed*,
Stephen Crane for the United States in *The Red Badge of
Courage*, and Giuseppe Lampedusa for Sicily in *The Leopard*.

The Malayan Trilogy is, in other words, conceived on the grand scale as a novel that recreates an historical time convincingly, authentically, imaginatively; it is indeed a novel that can be not unfavorably compared with those just listed.

Burgess's *Malayan Trilogy* is, however, not so much plotted as it is orchestrated. Themes are introduced, they are developed briefly, they appear later on somewhat varied, sometimes muted, but still insistent and vital. Major themes are supported by images and symbolical rendering, illustrated in dialogue and action, and enriched by metaphor and allusion. When Robert Loo sits down in *Beds in the East* to begin working on his violin concerto, Burgess suggests the musical planning of his novel: "The muse had told him peremptorily to start writing a violin concerto; that is to say, she had hurled themes at him, fully orchestrated, with a solo violin plunging in the foreground, and this solo part insisted on being rich in harmonics and intricate multiple stoppings. Behind these sharp images was a bigger, duller image which would only be fully realized when the work was complete, for it was the image of the work itself" (411).

The first installment of the trilogy, *Time for a Tiger,* introduces the central character, Victor Crabbe. The activity of the novel begins early in the morning: the *bilal* sings his prayer from the minaret. The religious theme, sounded first, appears and re-appears; but, at times, it is comically disguised in the antics of the Moslems, the Chinese, and the Malays. It is accompanied and sustained by water and jungle imagery. The first segment of the novel reaches its climax in the trip to the interior, a resolution is attempted, but is not fulfilled. Victor finds that he has managed to exorcise only a portion of the past. The flood-waters at the end of the first movement of the trilogy remind the reader again of the death-by-water theme introduced earlier in the knowledge that Victor had escaped drowning eight years before in the accident in which his first wife had, in fact, drowned. With the Christmas party, with the drinking of wine with Nabby Adams and Alladad Khan, the religious note sounded by the *bilal* at the novel's beginning is confirmed. But the theme is unfulfilled; it demands development, confirmation, and reso-lution.

The second installment of the trilogy, *The Enemy in the Blanket,* which is funnier and less insistent than the first installment, is a scherzo. The theme of history is introduced, and Crabbe's personal history becomes a counterpoint to the theme of Malayan history. He attempts to reconcile the disparate elements that he observes in the nation to his understanding of history. Infidelity, a minor theme in *Time for a Tiger,* reappears; but, less romantic and coarser, it suggests the lurking enemy. The Communist terrorists in the jungle introduce once again a note of fear into the pattern. But there is comic lightening in terms of the characters, the Abang, Ah Wing, and food-obsessed Herbert Talbot. Fenella attempts to bring Victor to a full appreciation of his unwillingness to live in the present when she pretends to be drowning in the sea. Stirred to action by her predicament, he finds that the memory of the cold English water is too strong. The resolution is approached, discouraged, left for completion later on. Still, the jungle imagery and the water imagery imply a mystical urgency; and the religious theme remains insistent.

The third installment reconciles the various patterns introduced by the first two books of the trilogy. *Beds in the East* insists on a resolution of the discrete themes. The trip to Gila is recalled in the trip to the Durian estate. The maimed foot and the cane given to Crabbe by Temple Haynes reveal religious connotations. The past encroaches more and more; the jungle and the river's water threaten again, as they had on the way to Gila. And then the stunning revelation is made: that Crabbe's first wife did not love him, that she was planning to leave him. The very music that she had recorded and given first to Victor, then to Costard, suggests a comic fugato. The fall into the river, the betrayal by Vythilingam, the death-by-water theme reach a tragic synthesis. In the short conclusion that follows, Victor is written off on the very day of the celebrations. Comically the word for "freedom" is *Merdeka!* Rosemary wonders why she hears a Frenchman yell only the first syllable. And the reader remembers that Crabbe too had been aware of the similarity between the Malay and the French words.

A discussion of the musical structuring of the novel could undoubtedly be carried on to greater meaning by anyone conversant with the technics of musical composition. Perhaps it is sufficient for the purpose of this study to indicate briefly the brilliance of Burgess's plan, the synthesis of musical patterns and the devices of the novel. The reader cannot help but conclude that this is the "bigger, duller image," "the image of the work itself," that Burgess had in mind. But the *Malayan Trilogy*, although formulated perhaps along the lines of a symphony, is still a novel and, therefore, subject to the criticism leveled at this form of art. There are many influences apparent and at work in the *Malayan Trilogy*, and chief among these is that of Joseph Conrad—the voyage of discovery, into the interior, into darkness; but Burgess's Malaya is no more Conrad's Archipelago than Bond Street is. E. M. Forster influences the trilogy and, to a certain extent, defines the mystical pattern that culminates in the "OM" that Crabbe recognizes at the end of *Beds in the East.*

Graham Greene, who insists on passionate pity, influences the characterization of Victor Crabbe, but again the influence is assimilated into the more compelling aspects of Burgess's protagonist. The flirting with time is vaguely reminiscent of both Joyce and Virginia Woolf, but once again the time theme is used in an original manner to point out and illustrate the various demands of the characterization and the plot. And surely Burgess's comic figures, especially Rosemary and the Abang, remind the reader of Evelyn Waugh's. But once again, it is the originality of the characters themselves, moving as they do hysterically, delightfully, grotesquely, and menacingly through the narrative, that enchant the reader. The reader may be aware of their provenance from Waugh, but they are ultimately Burgess's own; for, vital and real, they demand a life of their own, even outside the pages of the novel. Brilliantly, originally, Burgess uses the names of his characters to comic point. The "lingam," a Hindu manifestation of Siva, suggests the phallus; the *mahal* in Mahalingam suggests largeness; the *sunda* in Sundralingam, beauty; and vaidiam, consonant with Vythilingam's work as a veterinarian, suggests physician; the name Arumugam suggests the six faces of Murugan, the son of Siva.[5] And the symbolism of T. S. Eliot's *The Waste Land* and the *Four Quartets* is used in the novels to enrich, to remind, to comment on, to underscore, to suggest. The death-by-water theme, most dominant, brings into focus the trilogy's religious importunities, which are perhaps Burgess's chief concern.

For Burgess, like many before him, gives emphasis to the theory that all art is religious. Man's responsibility to his fellow man is what defines his humanity and perhaps determines his

salvation. There is also a strong implication in the trilogy that
the only morality left in the world is to be discovered in art.
Victor Crabbe is, therefore, a character of infinite appeal. His
name suggests victory, the apple, the scavenger. And the scapegoat theme, handled tenderly, emerges through him as one of
the most stunning aspects of the novel. Aristotelian peripety,
underscoring his attempts to accomplish the impossible, makes
Crabbe infinitely appealing and emphasizes an all-but-heroic
stature.

CHAPTER 4

Black and Ugly: Toward the West

I The Right to an Answer

IN his *Malayan Trilogy*, Anthony Burgess is successful in
describing the influx of the West into the Malayan world
partly because of the characterization of Victor Crabbe, the
protagonist. As Crabbe becomes more and more involved with
the East and as the reader begins to understand the claims of
politics, religion, and race upon a polyglot nation emerging
into the machine menace of the twentieth century, a certain
rapport is established between author and audience. Romantic,
bewildered, visionary, Crabbe moves into the arenas of politics,
religion, and race and develops, primarily through his reactions
to people caught in bewildering situations, a rich, comic appreciation of a world that is content with insanity and determined
on destruction. Crabbe lives and acts "as if" there were some
ultimate purpose behind existence, but he is fully aware of
life's ironic absurdities.

As a result of the characterization, the reader discovers quite
soon that the real problems underlying communication and
understanding between East and West are not so much ideo-
logical as theological: that the relationship of man to God and
thence to man forms a religious complex that needs not so
much explanation as appreciation. No scene in Burgess's trilogy
better illustrates this point than the comic "bridge" party, the
device by which Crabbe intends to plant the seeds of pride in
an indigenous art among the disparate groups of Malaya. The
themes, then, that inform the action of the *Malayan Trilogy*
are religious: commitment and responsibility, guilt and personal
redemption. The jargon of present-day Existential thought can
be employed in this regard to explain and justify: Existentialism
can even be used to assess the heroism of the protagonist, and
Crabbe does come perilously close to achieving heroic stature
in the course of the novel.

But Crabbe, preoccupied as he is with guilt, reflects a religious
more than a philosophical concern. Indeed, in Burgess's world
it soon becomes apparent that all actions ultimately reflect a
concern with man as a creature capable of performing good and
evil actions. Sometimes this theological preoccupation is symbolically implied; sometimes it is belligerently portrayed; but
more often than not, it is disguised in comic dress. Nevertheless,
the final consideration remains religious. Crabbe's death in the
Mayalan Trilogy, enigmatic, poignant, symbolically and artis-
tically appropriate, implies but does not insist upon a theological
comment, as does Scobie's final action in Graham Greene's *The
Heart of the Matter*. Whether Crabbe stumbles accidentally,
his cane unable to support him, or whether he falls into the
river's waters intentionally, is assuredly a problem of theological
purport; but Burgess wisely does not insist, and it is unnecessary
for him to do so. The symbolism of death by water portrays
tellingly enough the religious aspects of the scene. If the reader
feels forced to make a judgment, he does so at his own risk.

In *The Right to an Answer* (1960),[1] the concern with the
nature of responsibility is extended and achieves a new comic
ambiance through the sybaritic narrator, J. W. Denham. And
again the reader is introduced to a world that is at once real
and allegorical. Like the *Malayan Trilogy*, *The Right to an
Answer* is an extremely witty book. Like the trilogy, its parts,
which at first appear disparate, nevertheless cohere, primarily
because of the originality of the characters, the ingeniousness
of the comic devices, and the "black humor" that both horrifies
and delights.

Richly textured, *The Right to an Answer* is "a study of
provincial England, as seen by a man on leave from the East,
with special emphasis on the decay of traditional values in an
affluent society."[2] The influence of Vladimir Nabokov is apparent
on Burgess's art in the emphasis that Burgess places on language
as he forces it to enlarge character and add dimension to his
religious theme. In a review of Andrew Field's *Nabokov: His
Art in Life* (1967), Burgess comments on Nabokov's method
and throws light on his own in devising a novel. Speaking of
Quilty, the antagonist of *Lolita*, Burgess observes: "The enemy
Quilty (*Qu'il t'y mène*—let him take you there) opens up a
surrealistic world where identities are unsure, the enemy is the
alter ego, action is dream. Each new reading of the book . . .

invites warier treading."[3] And he then observes that Nabokov, in reacting to the plain style—Hemingway's and Maugham's—reminds the reader that plainness engenders emasculation of language; Nabokov "shows that pedantry can be a kind of dandyism, and that ecstasy and rich humor are not really strange bedfellows" (*The New York Times Book Review*, July 2, 1967, p. 20).

The use of the alter ego, of action as dream, and of language as enlarging upon and as leading into ritual, each underscored by hilarity and grotesque comedy, are, indeed, devices borrowed from Nabokov; but again, as in Burgess's earlier books, the demands of the theme determine the originality of the book. The subterranean life of the novel is what distinguishes it: a seeming slip, "communionism" for "communism"; a pattern of drinking and eating, suggesting the Roman Catholic mass; gestures of benediction; and a gangster-God justifying an anti-heroic protagonist.

In his Malayan trilogy, Burgess introduced a Westerner into the East; in *The Right to an Answer*, he introduces a Ceylonese into the English suburban world of wife-swapping, pub-drinking, "telly" viewing, and film-star worshiping. The world that Mr. Raj enters is the world of English suburbia, a world dominated by television but a world still capable of provoking tragedy.

The narration of the *Malayan Trilogy* is in the third person, but the action is chiefly portrayed through Crabbe's romantic eyes; history and change are his preoccupations. The narration of *The Right to an Answer* is first person; and it becomes important to understand the protagonist if any assessment of the novel's theme is to be arrived at: "I'm telling this story mainly for my own benefit. I want to clarify in my own mind the nature of the mess that so many people seem to be in nowadays," writes J. W. Denham on the first page. "I lack the mental equipment and the training and the terminology to say whether the mess is social or religious or moral..." (7). The social, religious, or moral mess that is England is what Burgess confronts the reader with in the course of the novel's activities; and he places his fine focus on adultery and responsibility.

On leave from his well-paying job in Japan, Denham, the narrator, finds himself in the suburbs of a large midland city visiting his father, a retired printer. Early in the account of his visit to his father, Denham observes that the church spire interferes with television reception; but his father does not mind, especially since his sight is failing. Denham also observes that the life of the community centers on either the "telly" or the pub; and, of the two, the pub is preferable because the people there, even though they come from the sterile suburb, do drink Babycham and bitter, and do go through the motions of living. The Black Swan or Mucky Duck, presided over by Ted Arden, whose resemblance to Shakespeare is explained by his descent from Shakespeare's mother's family, stands "in a pocket of village"; it is "the dirty speck round which the pearly suburb had woven itself," "a tiny reservation for aborigines" (12). The setting of the novel is terrifying, surreal.

After watching the "telly," whose images produce doppel-gangers "that seem to stand a step behind," Denham and his father make their way to the pub. There Denham observes a version of musical chairs called "wife-swapping." He meets Winter the printer, whose name he immediately divines as Winterbottom (Cold Arse). Then he meets Winter's wife, Alice, who is in the company of Charlie Whittier, Jack Brownlow, and Brownlow's wife; Denham recognizes this group as a Saturday-night foursome. Ted Arden, the Mucky Duck's host, occasions a reverie concerning the nature of British social and communal life. Denham knows that he himself is rich enough to stock his father's house with all the drinks of Ted Arden's pub, to install a small bar if he wants to: "But it is recognized in England that home drinking is no real pleasure. We pray in a church and booze in a pub: profoundly sacerdotal at heart, we need a host in both places to preside over us. In Catholic churches as in continental bars the host is there all the time. But the Church of England kicked out the Real Presence and the licensing laws give the landlord a terrible sacramental power" (21-22).

When Ted Arden asks Denham to stay behind after the others have left, Denham feels that Ted is giving him grace, holding back death, and making him a lordly gift of extra life. In the presence of Hieronymus Bosch-like grotesques—Selwyn, an imbecile with the gift of prophecy; Cedric, the barboy; Arden himself and his wife, Veronica; and a gruff boxer—Ted Arden invites Denham to pay for a bottle of mysterious liquor whose Cyrillic label indicates that it might be Russian vodka. "I reckon the Russians is as good as what we are," growls the boxer. "What is this Communionism? It's everybody doing their best for every-

one else, the way I see it" (23). The liquor is ceremonially
dispensed amid talk of "R.C.'s" and "C. of E.'s" and "Primitive
Methodists." What the drinking scene amounts to is a black
mass. The Mucky Duck speaks obliquely of the Holy Ghost.
Drunk on the liquor, Denham borrows Arden's sacerdotal office
and delivers a sermon on adultery. He and Winterbottom leave
the pub together to seek out the adulterous Alice so that she
can give her husband the house key. Another key is thrown to
the brawlers from a bedroom, but it is not Winterbottom's.
Wife-swapping appears to be a way of life in the suburbs.
Denham, however, has given a name to Alice's activities and
by doing so has set in motion events of tragic consequence.

At his sister Beryl's house, Denham meets Everett, a one-time
Georgian poet, a friend of Harold Munro, and writer once for
the *Blast* and *Adelphi* but presently on the literary page of the
local *Hermes*. Beryl, a Dickensian caricature, plans for Denham
to give Everett several hundred pounds so that he can have a
volume of his collected poems privately printed. Denham is
not averse to the idea, especially after he has met Imogen,
Everett's daughter, who is a marvel of comic obscenity: "Damn
it all, the least you can do is spend a couple of hundred quid
on my father. It's the job of the rich to help the poor men of
genius, isn't it?" she says (54).

When a business involvement forces Denham to leave England
temporarily, he meets in Ceylon a gangster in the heroin racket
and also the incomparable Mr. Raj. To the gangster, Len,
Denham tells the story of his evening in London before flying
to Colombo. He had been approached by a girl and had gone
to a hotel with her; she had asked him to pay her in advance,
then had bilked him of five pounds by leaving through the
bathroom and the adjacent empty bedroom. Len, who listens
with fascination, professes not to believe in violence, only in
punishment; and the concept of the gangster-God, broached in
A Vision of Battlements, is expressed through him: "[V]iolence
is a different thing from punishment. You mustn't be too easy
on people. It only encourages them to carry on with the same
lark. Give them a good sharp punishment, something that'll
last. It's only for the good of humanity, when all's said and
done. And for their own good too" (68). To this statement,
Denham remarks that Len ought to be God. Len agrees that,

if he were God, he would do things differently; and he raises his fingers in a parody of benediction as he speaks.

Mr. Raj introduces himself to Denham, claims the kinship of the British Commonwealth, and makes Denham responsible for introducing him into the society that Denham is returning to, that of the Midland town where, coincidentally, Mr. Raj is to pursue his studies in the university. "Apollo in frozen milk chocolate, though the eyes melted and burned," his body scooped and passionate, like Charlie Whittier's, Mr. Raj, dressed in a superb sharkskin tuxedo, tells Denham with a "wide fanatic smile" that he is going to the university to write a thesis to be called "Popular Conceptions of Racial Differentiation" (70-71). He asks Denham to help him penetrate into the folds and recesses of the better English society. "I doubt not," he says, "that with your help I shall soon be *persona grata*" (71).

Through a series of comic involvements, Mr. Raj is introduced to the clientele of the Black Swan and to the adulterous quartet. Soon he is living with Denham's father and occupying Denham's room; the doppelganger finds himself in possession of the white man's father, whom he tends and cares for as though he were his own; but, feeding him rich curries that both enchant and intoxicate the elderly man, he finally brings about his death. At the Black Swan, Raj is forced to defend himself against Brownlow, whom he knocks down expertly several times. And, while Ted Arden is showing off a collection of weapons and old books, Raj manages to steal a small gun, which he promises Denham that he will use only to intimidate those who attempt to bother him on the streets at night.

Raj confesses bewilderment concerning English ways and surprise at the amount of blood that is involved in Christianity; for blood is something to wash off, not to be washed in. "I come here to study ineffable and imponderable problems of race relationships," he says to the Denhams. "So far I have had mixed career. Fights and insults, complete lack of sexual sustenance—most necessary to men in prime of life—and inability to find accommodation commensurate with social position and academic attainments" (125). During his first evening in the Denhams' home, Mr. Raj is moved by the moment; and he makes a toast to Love: "Love, yes, that is the answer. We not fear, ever, if only we have in our hearts, if only we give and, in reciprocity, receive, this greatest of all human treasures" (133). Believing

himself in love with Alice Winterbottom, Mr. Raj is confused
by English women who, promising everything and giving nothing,
keep men panting.

When Denham returns from Colombo to England in Mr. Raj's
company, he discovers that Everett's daughter Imogen has run
off to London with Winterbottom; and he wonders what Imogen
can see in the sulky little printer. When Imogen proposes to
be Denham's mistress, he pretends to be shocked by her proposi-
tion, although he does acknowledge her attraction for him.
"Allright, I shan't make you another offer. You've had it now.
But you'll be to blame if I start doing anything worse," Imogen
says (90). And Denham answers characteristically, "I accept
no blame for anything. You ought to spend a nice quiet evening
sorting out your own moral position. . . . You can leave me out
of it" (90-91). Denham does, however, lend the errant lovers
seventy-five pounds, accepting responsibility only for their physical well-being. Money for Denham is a means of avoiding
involvement. "There are no free gifts nowadays: everything
has to be paid for. And time, which costs nothing, costs the
most," he observes early in the book (21).

To Denham, who returns to Japan by ship, Raj sends messages
and letters begging for clarification of English ways, asking
advice about the possibility of platonic relationships. Denham
delays answering, primarily because he does not want to acknowledge responsibility for Raj's difficulties, until he can do so no
longer. He finally sends a cryptic cablegram, which Raj interprets
to mean that such relationships are not possible among men
and women of normal passions. But Alice continues to lead
him on, and Raj continues to care for Denham's father. It does
occur to Denham that he receives no real news of his father—
even a line or two in Raj's letters would be some indication of
the old man's health; but again, not wishing to be overly involved, he neglects to inquire about the old man.

In Singapore, on Bugis Street, Denham again encounters the
gangster Len. After proclaiming an admiration for Graham
Greene's novels, Len continues the explanation, begun in Ceylon,
of his moral code: "you could only get close to God if you
really got down to the real dirt, so to speak" (147). The "real
thing," Len believes, is justice, and he demonstrates himself to
be a perverted Manichaean with a God complex: "[I]t seems to
me that you can't have a pair of scales with one pan in this

world and the other in the next. That's where I part company
with God.... [P]eople have got to be taught here and now.
That way every one of us is a little bit of God. That's what God
is, perhaps, just all of us" (148).

Denham learns that Len and several of his cohorts had
followed while in London a girl who had skipped out on her
client through an adjoining bedroom without having given service for the five pounds that she had requested in advance. The
girl, Imogen, had been beaten up by Len and his gangster
friends: "A couple of teeth is as good a punishment as any"
(151). Furious at Len's "trying to be God," Denham threatens
to knock out several of the gangster's teeth. "It isn't as if I've
done anything wrong," argues Len; "I just put the balance
right, that's all. If you did that to me I'd have to do something
of the same sort to you. And so it would have to go on. You'd
have to learn about justice too" (151). Denham is made uncomfortably aware of the fact that a harm done to one is
done to all, and that to deny this fact is to deny life itself.

Summoned back to London by Ted Arden to attend his
father's funeral, Denham confronts Mr. Raj, who tells Denham
that he loved his father. But Denham blames him for the old
man's death, implying as he does so that he does not consider
the black man the equal of the white. When Raj challenges him,
Denham replies that, although the men of the East use the
words "love," "equality," and "brotherhood," they interpret the
words irresponsibly. "I have failed to make contact...failed,
failed, failed," says Mr. Raj (190).

Mr. Raj goes to Alice and finds her with Winterbottom who,
taking Denham's advice, has returned to her. Raj kills Winterbottom, using the gun he had borrowed from Ted Arden. Unable
to tear her neighbors away from their "telly" during peak
viewing hours to witness the real death taking place next door,
Alice comes to Denham. When Denham finds Raj, Raj kills
himself in front of Denham, and he winks as he does so. To
Raj, a Hindu who believes in the oneness of life, death is perhaps a joke.

The novel's theme is expressed by the poet Everett who comments obliquely on the passionate activities that make up the
plot. With Imogen returned to him, Everett plans to begin
writing a new kind of poetry, "A poetry which says that none of
us really has a right to an answer" (181). Everett explains that

the question that demands an answer is ultimately one question and that, although everyone knows what that question is, it is still not easy to define. The reader remembers that earlier in the novel Mr. Raj had spoken of love and understanding.

Denham, aware of himself and of his unwillingness to participate in the activities of life, reminds the reader uncomfortably of Conrad's Axel Heyst, but he lacks Heyst's true gallantry. Denham knows himself to be a pretender: "Thank God I have never been committed, as a salesman in Africa or Asia, to any philosophy of ultimate identification through closer and closer and deeper and deeper contact, over which to grow, at length, grey with frustration.... There was just this man, J. W. Denham, buying and selling, alone and content to be so, except in work, play, bed, his shadow moving over exotic backcloths ..." (193). Considering himself above and apart from the world of "telly" viewers, the zombies and the madmen, Denham has learned to pretend contact, to listen and to acquiesce to what he does not care to understand. The world of the picture tube reveals flat characters, wobbling shadows; yet he himself is no more substantial than those images that he despises.

After his father's funeral, Denham returns to his work in Japan. His mistress has left him, perhaps frightened into life by the real world that accosted her one dark night in the disguise of street hoodlums. He is soon visited by Ted Arden and his wife who are making a trip on the money that Everett has gotten for them by selling the early *Hamlet* quarto that he and Denham had discovered among Arden's family relics on the night of Denham's father's funeral. The section of the play to which Denham had turned to judge the value of the quarto had been, aptly, the "To be or not to be" speech.

After taking leave of Ted Arden and Veronica, Denham looks at himself seriously in the mirror. There is no doppelganger to confuse the picture, as there had been on his father's television set. What he sees is a self-indulgent, disgustingly hirsute, balding man. The unloving eyes and the hard mouth displease him. As he thinks back over the events of the previous several months, he concludes that his life of "not-wishing-to-be-involved," though comfortable, is empty. And he concludes that the life that Mr. Raj, who had come too soon "for the blending," had contended with—"the troubled ocean" in the *Hamlet* quarto—is at least a means of measuring a man's moral being.

The *Malayan Trilogy* deals with commitment, and dedication to the Malayans inspires in Victor Crabbe an all-but-accomplished heroism; *The Right to an Answer* deals with the theme of noninvolvement and loneliness. Both novels are, however, concerned with guilt and responsibility. The question that deserves to be answered is asked by Mr. Raj; and, at the novel's end, when Denham turns to Mr. Raj's unfinished manuscript about the problems of race relationships, he becomes aware of the answer: *"Trust is love, credit is a form of love, reliance on the police force or army of a state is also a form of love.... Love seems inevitable, necessary, as normal and as easy a process as respiration, but unfortunately"* (218). The manuscript ends with the word "unfortunately," without punctuation.

The Right to an Answer, more straightforward in manner than the *Malayan Trilogy,* manages, by means of juxtaposing comic scenes with scenes of social and religious purport, to suggest the necessity of formulating an answer for the question posed by the Ceylonese Raj. The expression which Mr. Raj hears as "bitter fun" instead of as "a bit of fun," is used several times in the course of the novel to define the peculiar effect produced by Raj on the people who meet him; the expression also defines the tone and feeling that the novel formulates. From Raj's first comic appearance, in his superbly cut tuxedo made of sharkskin material, he delights and enchants the reader. His function as alter ego involves him much more intimately in the ways of British life than an objective observer should be involved. That he has come too soon for "blending," as Burgess calls integration, is the point that lends the novel both its comic and its tragic value. That Burgess should risk the theme to a comic vehicle is not so remarkable when his indebtedness to Nabokov is appreciated.

What is remarkable is that Burgess succeeds as well as he does. The pub as the center of human activity is symbolically appropriate, especially when Burgess describes those who linger on its outskirts: the imbeciles who leer down at weed patches, the cocks that crow all day, the little girls in pinafores who "schnockle" over half-eaten apples, and the boys who all seem to have cleft palates. The workmen in the pub, Selwyn and Cedric, an imbecile and a near-imbecile, also enhance the surrealistic quality that informs the symbolism; and the fact that Selwyn was born with a caul and has the gift of prophecy intensifies the feeling of religious obliquity touched upon when Denham remarks that the church spire interferes with television reception. The wobbling shadows of the television sets form phosphorescent contrasts to the passionate activities of Denham's alter ego, Mr. Raj. Yet all the activity is related by a hollow man. Black and white dominate in the novel; there is very little color; and the sun figures not at all.

What disturbs the reader, however, is Burgess's means of establishing the values of a previous age—through the character of grasping Ted Arden, a descendant of the Ardens of Shakespeare biography. The gratuitous discovery of the *Hamlet* quarto is a device necessary to bring the Ardens into Japan, where Denham is at home; and this visit is necessary to acquaint the reader fully with Denham's failure. When Denham says that, upon retirement, he will return to England and marry Imogen, the reader knows that Denham has not learned what Heyst had learned: that a habit long lived cannot be broken. Imogen is a dream out of Shakespeare, but Denham is a wobbling shadow. Perhaps if he had knocked out the gangster's teeth, as he threatened to do when he was told about Imogen's beating, he might have discovered his humanity, just as Heyst had discovered his when he had obeyed Lena's command to save her from Schomberg's evil.

II The Doctor Is Sick

Anyone reading Anthony Burgess's novels eventually asks himself, Haven't I covered this ground before? The answer is invariably, Yes! For Burgess does indeed borrow from both his contemporaries and those writers of the past he most admires. But what is equally true is that he transmutes all that he touches by virtue of his wit and his comic brilliance.

Published in England in 1960, *The Doctor Is Sick*[4] reminds the reader of Kingsley Amis's *Lucky Jim* as well as of Henry Fielding's *Tom Jones*. And the protagonist's search for self-awareness through the labyrinths of the mind reminds him, inevitably, of James Joyce's *Ulysses*, as does the emphasis that Burgess places on words as such. Indeed in this novel, perhaps more than in any that has come before, the use of the word approximates a sacramental act, much as it does in the works of Joyce. The wandering hero of the novel also reminds the

reader of Dickens's Nicholas Nickleby; and the twin Jewish
brothers, Leo and Harry Stone, suggest the Cheeryble brothers
gone berserk. The protagonist's peregrinations in London low-
life seem to owe a great deal to Dickens's underworld; but,
ultimately, the comic episodes are Burgess's own, used here to
balance a metaphysical dimension.

The Doctor Is Sick is Burgess's foray into the picaresque
novel, but it is equally an attempt to consider the nature of
illusion and reality. The conventions of the rogue novel are used
as an excuse to allow Burgess to study both the symbolical and
the historical aspects of language and to consider the values
of contemporary civilization. The comic episodes become devices
that allow the protagonist to confront aspects of himself as
he wanders between the worlds of reality and of nightmare,
and that, incidentally, introduce the reader to a marvelous
variety of dialect and slang.

The protagonist of the novel is Edwin Spindrift, and his name
suggests the pattern of the book. Edwin spins the episodes and
then drifts within them. His name is also used to imply various
aspects of merchandising, suggesting as it does detergents and
washing machines, as well as the sea. "There's a poem by Kipling,
I believe, that uses the word finely," says an old clergyman to
Edwin toward the novel's end. "Something something something
shall fail not from the face of it, something something spindrift
and the fulmar flying free" (209).

Like The Right to an Answer before it, The Doctor Is Sick
plays on the theme of marital infidelity. In The Right to an
Answer, Denham and Winterbottom went into the streets of
the suburb to look for Alice; and Denham had spoken the
word "adultery," thus isolating Alice's "sin" and setting the
pattern of the novel's action. In The Doctor Is Sick, Edwin
Spindrift thinks constantly about his wife Sheila and about
whether or not he should leave her. Like Denham before him,
he plays with words, lavishes affection on them, but does not
fully understand their value as symbols.

Edwin—on leave from his job as a teacher of language in
Moulmein, Burma, to have an illness that affects his olfactory
nerves and his libido diagnosed—finds himself manipulated by
technicians in starched white hospital uniforms until he feels
that he can no longer stand their tortures. After several spinal
taps, after air is pumped into his brain, his illness is diagnosed

as a brain tumor. Sheila, unwilling to spend too much time with him, sends in her place a number of eccentrics she meets while playing shove ha'penny and darts at the Anchor pub. Charlie, the window washer; 'Ippo, the illiterate board carrier; Nigel, the painter; Les and his foul-mouthed North African-Spanish mistress, Carmen—these lead Edwin by degrees to the Stone twins and their German mistress, Renate; Renate's prostitute daughters who by day share a bed and by night all their adventures; Bob Courage, a kettle (cheap wristwatch) racketeer with a taste for flagellation; Mr. Chasper, Spindrift's superior in London who rescues Edwin from Bob Courage in a men's rest room; Jack Thanatos, an old school chum who wears vine leaves in his hair; and many, many other Dickensian characters gone absolutely wild.

Given a sedative after being fed stewed brains and after having his head shaved preparatory to his operation, Spindrift decides to leave the hospital and to look for his wife. The ambiguity—whether the adventures that he encounters are real or the results of an hallucination before, during, and after the operation—is the point of the novel. For the book asks what is real, what is appearance? Spindrift is involved in one hilarious episode after another, and each of the episodes in some way reflects the concerns that he takes into the hospital: his wife's promiscuity; his interest in words and the fine points of linguistics; his virility—in other words, his knowledge of himself. At the novel's end, the reader wonders not so much whether the comic episodes are hallucinations but whether Edwin has learned what he needs to know about himself and his commitment to life. Indeed, the reader is not even certain that Edwin is in the world of the living; for he dresses and leaves the hospital to search out Thanatos, who may or may not exist, and whose name means death.

The comic episode that ties all the others together is the contest for the Bald Adonis of Greater London, a contest that Spindrift with his recently shaved head wins easily. After receiving the prize of ten pounds, instead of the hundred he had expected, Spindrift speaks a foul word into a television microphone and thereby achieves a sort of immortality. He leaves the theater where the contest had been held and walks into a glossy Edwardian hotel where he is recognized by his old school friend, Jack Thanatos, a wine merchant, who invites him to a party that turns out to be a bacchanal. Tired from the activities of the day, unable to speak as he should, Edwin accepts his friend's offer of a bed for the night. In looking for the hotel room, he finds Sheila in bed with a stranger. Edwin faints; he then awakens in a new ward in the hospital, the operation over, and to what may or may not be reality.

When Sheila comes, she tells him that she is leaving him, returning to Burma and to Jeff Fairlove, whose name, like Spindrift's, assumes symbolical importance within the narrative. Edwin attempts to explain to Sheila that his adventures, real or imagined, have made him aware of his humanity, or lack of it, that in searching for her, through the mazes of his sub-conscious perhaps, he had been admitting his love for her: "These last few days brought me out of touch with words as words. And it seemed that coming into contact with life made me into a liar, a thief, a whoremaster, a cheat, a man on the run. But you say that these last few days never happened. So that I'm still the same" (219). Edwin objects feebly when Sheila maintains that it is a sin that a man should love only his work; but she concedes, gently, that it is the only sin he had ever committed; to her, it is, however, the unforgivable sin.

The point of the discourse, as Edwin realizes, is not so much that he loves his work but that he has used his work as a refuge from the demands of life in the world that Sheila is a part of. She leaves the hospital and returns several minutes later, ostensibly for her handbag, to tell Edwin that a man with vine leaves around his head wants to see him as soon as possible. Whether the latter part of the scene actually occurs is not altogether clear. Edwin dresses and leaves the hospital. He meets 'Ippo, who says, "Workin' nights now, see. The End, that's what it is, the end" (224).

The episodes of the novel depend on the factor of time for a good deal of their meaning; one episode surrealistically fuses into another, very much like the sequences of a long and complicated nightmare. Whether or not these episodes cover the full complement of clock time that the narrative suggests depends on the reader's accepting them as real or hallucinatory. In either case, Burgess's method relies on the reader's awareness that Spindrift is ill, that his sense of reality is, as is his sense of smell, impaired by the illness. The searching out of the meaning of time within the novel reveals the metaphysical implications of the episodes as well as Burgess's indebtedness to Joyce's associational method.

Spindrift notices, soon after Sheila's envoy 'Ippo, leaves him, that his wristwatch is gone. The wristwatch is an expensive one, given to him by Sheila, who soon reveals that Jeff Fairlove had given it to her. When Edwin leaves the hospital to search for Sheila, he feels strangely vulnerable; and he thinks of himself in a pram, as he was in a photograph his mother had had framed for the front room—"little Edwin with sharp mistrustful eyes, a jowl, and a day's growth of beard" (67). He gathers his clothes, descends into the hospital's cellar, and leaves by way of a window. On the street he soon notices magazines with strange titles: *"Valour; Act; Oh! ... Air, Pride, Plume, Here?"* The titles, of course, are drawn from Gerard Manley Hopkins's poem "The Windhover," and they stop just short of the key word "Buckle." A train station soon becomes a Gothic cathedral, "skinned over with grime" (77). Edwin notices headlines: the death of a jive girl at a wedding is given greater prominence than the thousand Japanese who have been made homeless by an earthquake.[5] He makes socks out of the newspaper, and he holds tight to his passport, his link with his conscious identity.

He locates the hotel where Sheila had been staying. "Here is staying nobody of such name," he is told by a man carrying a fish. The hotel proprietor adds, "I wouldn't have her any longer, and you can tell her from me that it's no good her trying to come back under another name" (80). The search to find Sheila is, however, merely the conscious motive that propels Edwin on his journey through the seamy side of London life; the subconscious motive is his search for identity. Thus the passport assumes double importance. He buys matches with the few pennies he has left, feeling that a man is better off having an element in his pocket; he thinks of Prometheus.

Off Great Russell Street, he encounters 'Ippo, who is carrying boards that spell out biblical texts. When Edwin demands his watch, 'Ippo, negligently named after Saint Augustine of Hippo, denies knowing Spindrift. When a gust of wind blows a piece of newspaper onto 'Ippo's board, it hides all the text except the words "There is no God" (88). A policeman comes upon the scene, and Edwin thinks of him as the state's symbol for original sin. Still looking for Sheila, he goes to the Anchor pub, where he encounters the Stone twins who explain why

they look after the German prostitute Renate. "Guilt," says
Harry Stone, "Ve Germans gave ve Jews a bleedin' rotten time"
(96). The vague reference "ve" is intentional; the Stone twins
care for Renate because after the war they had themselves given
several German women a "bleedin' rotten time." Guilt is universal.

Soon, in the Stones' illegal club, Edwin encounters Bob
Courage, a racketeer who does a brisk business with "kettles,"
and the factor of time is again introduced. To prevent the police
from arresting the assemblage for illegal possession of alcohol,
Edwin is asked to lecture; and he begins to speak on folk
etymology. He stumbles over the terms "penthouse," "prim-
rose," "Jerusalem artichoke," "causeway," and "chalk"—the same
terms he had stumbled over before fainting the first time in
Burma. There is one significant difference, however; in Burma he
had said, on awakening, "While we honour none but the horizontal one"; in London he says, "Let us praise while we can . . .
the vertical man" (Cf. 11, 112). The horizontal and the vertical
references reinforce the religious dimension suggested by "The
Windhover" and 'Ippo's signs.

Bob Courage develops a liking for Spindrift, deciding that
Edwin's "kinky" tastes coincide with his own. He kidnaps
Edwin; there is a long loaf of French bread and two "nickers'"
worth of smoked salmon in Bob's car, again symbolically suggesting sex and religion. When Edwin manages to elude Bob
temporarily by going into the cellar of Covent Garden Opera
House, he is given a costume for a part in an opera. He watches
a game in which the content of Salome's basket is thrown about.
He steals a wig, leaves the opera, and finds Bob waiting for him.
At Bob's apartment, Edwin climbs five flights of stairs—the
first mention of ascent—a meaning of which is "to surface."

An old heavy door that once protected a "posh" establishment yields before Bob's key reluctantly, and Spindrift is introduced to Bob's "kinky" taste in flagellation. Soon he finds
himself whipping and kicking Bob and enjoying doing both.
A knock at the door interrupts the proceeding; Bob leaves,
ostensibly to peddle his cheap watches; and Spindrift vandalizes
the already filthy flat. He throws out all of Bob's whips, except
one, which he plans to use on Bob as a surprise weapon when
he returns. He grows frightened; and suddenly he begins to
understand himself:

He had lived too much with words and not what the words stood for.... Apart from its accidents of sound, etymology and lexical definition, did he really know the meaning of any one word? Love, for instance. Interesting, that collocation of sounds: the clear allo-phone of the voiced divided phoneme gliding to that newest of all English vowels.... Let him loose in the real world, where words are glued to things, and see what he did: stole, swore, lied, committed acts of violence on things and people. He had never been sufficiently interested in words, that was the whole trouble. (133)

Each of the major scenes of the novel, unified by Edwin's search for his wife and by Bob Courage's pursuit of him, suggest the chase motif common to early motion pictures. There is a Marx Brothers-Keystone Cops aspect to the various scenes; they are bound together by the hilarity and suspense they provoke.

An examination of the details of each episode inevitably yields, however, an appreciation of the metaphysical dimension, the novel's real concern. Each detail is based in some way on Spindrift's immediate problems—his illness and his fear of death (bringing about Jack Thanatos), his wife's infidelity, and his evasion of life that is disguised as a love of words. Each episode is rich in linguistic detail and full of comic delight, as Burgess transcribes the speech of the Yiddish-Cockney Stone brothers, the German-Cockney Renate, the North African-Spanish-Cockney Carmen, and that of the numerous other characters too. Although the episodes are rich in comic and human detail, they do more importantly pattern the self-discovery in which Edwin is involved. Through the scenes, interpreted either as actually occurring or as hallucinations, Edwin encoun-ters the various aspects of himself in the situations that unfold dizzyingly before him. The fact that the novel ends ambiguously is simply another means of registering once again the pertinence of the major theme—the difficulty of determining what is real and what is illusory.

The major argument of *The Doctor Is Sick* considers the disparities between truth and illusion, reality and nightmare. Second to this major consideration is the theme of guilt and responsibility which is mirrored not only in Edwin's confronta-tions with the Stone brothers but also in his Joyce-inspired call to the sons of Adam in Edenville, made from a telephone booth early in the morning of his escape from the hospital. 'Ippo's religious texts reveal man's dilemma—the problem of remaining alive and human. The theme of free will and choice is also developed in the novel, primarily through Edwin's appreciation of his wife's oblique morality: Sheila believes that a sin against the Holy Ghost is total, ultimate, and unforgivable when, "of one's own free will in spiritual intimacy with another," it is committed. Edwin fears that, since his libido has failed, his marriage will also fail; for, with no choice to make, Sheila's right to choose his or another's bed is denied her (17-18).

All in all, *The Doctor Is Sick*—comically and suspensefully contrived within the conventions of the picaresque novel—reveals the growing artistry of the novelist. The central character is marvelously conceived, ironically developed, and sympathetically portrayed. There is a greater artistic security in this novel than was apparent in the highly plotted *The Right to an Answer;* and the "black" comedy, insistently funny and ferociously witty, sustains with decision and authority the metaphysical theme. The expression "bitter fun" can still be used to define the feeling of the novel, but the bitter fun is more equally balanced against the theme; there is perhaps not so much bitterness as there is fun. In Spindrift, Burgess further suggests the dilemma of contemporary man. In the brilliant bacchanalian scene with Jack Thanatos and Mr. Thallasus, whose name means "sea," Spindrift gives voice to his deepest wish when he says, *"Apothanein thelo"* ("I want to die").

But what is even more remarkable about the novel is Burgess's marvelous facility with words as they are forced to reveal the subterranean dimension of the novel. Again the eating and drinking scenes suggest religious meanings, for they frequently appear as little more than darkly disguised masses. The anti-heroic exploits of the protagonist, furthermore, direct the reader to comment upon the religious implications.

III   Devil of a State

In many ways, *Devil of a State*[6] reminds the reader of Evelyn Waugh's *Black Mischief* and the closing sequences of *A Handful of Dust*; but, as in Burgess's previous novel, the similarities come to little because the plot devices and ironic manipulations are marked by a comic gravity that can only be defined as original Burgess. The cannibalism and head shrinking, so reminiscent of Basil Seal's adventures in Azania, are used as metaphors within an eccentrically plotted novel[7] to remind the reader, grotesquely, that all men are implicated in an aboriginal calamity. An ape in workingman's clothes moves through the activities of the novel carrying the protagonist's photograph for the same reason—to remind the reader how far from and yet how near to primitive man he stands. Perhaps for these reasons the novel is dedicated to Graham Greene.

`Published in 1961, *Devil of a State* employs two epigraphs, one from Giuseppe Giusti's "l'Europeo," and the other from I Corinthians, to set the time and introduce the primary theme. Loosely translated, the epigraph from Giusti implies the double-edged irony that pervades the novel's plot:

> . . . Those priests have predicted
> that the country step by step
> will soon become civilized;
> but it will remain doltish.

And the epigraph from Corinthians suggests the principal thematic consideration, marriage and its responsibilities: "It is better to marry than to burn."

The action of the novel is determined by what can be called plot points. There are three major divisions; and, although each sequence culminates in the same climax, each allows its action to veer eccentrically into the activity of the other two major divisions. There are, furthermore, several minor plots at work; and the action resulting from these subplots also veers into that of the three major divisions. What appears to be confusion and chaos, superficially a means of suggesting the moral and legal ambiguities of the state of Dunia, appears upon consideration to be more correctly a means of suggesting how all men are tied to one another. The head shrinkers and cannibals who remain in the background, away from civilization, become, in the context of the novel's "religious" dimension, the enforcers of the gangster-God, the force that Len personifies in *The Right to an Answer*; the force that Ennis, before him, in *A Vision of Battlements,* acknowledges.

With the character of Lydgate, the protagonist of *Devil of a State,* Burgess portrays still another facet of the antihero. About Ennis in *A Vision of Battlements* there remains the Byronic aura, the social rebel at odds with the inhuman machinery of army bureaucracy; and the bulk of the reader's sentiment is for him, even as he induces the native boy to vandalize the billets of the officers who fail to treat him fairly. In the Malayan trilogy, Crabbe had been cast in a romantic mold; the theme of commitment had vitiated the antiheroic aspects of the characterization; and Crabbe remains sympathetic to the end. In *The Right to an Answer,* Burgess employs the device of alter egos: although Denham is the narrator and appears to be the protagonist, he is in effect his own observer—the action is determined by Raj, who, ironically, kills two people in the name of love. In *The Doctor Is Sick,* Spindrift's antiheroism is mitigated by the fact of his illness. Flirting with metaphysical concepts—time and life, love and death—the novel describes the "antiheroic" and comic exploits of the protagonist; but Burgess consistently intrudes the sympathetic, rational man to offset the irresponsibility engendered in his protagonist's antiheroic actions.

With Frank Lydgate in *Devil of a State,* although there are several moments in the course of the novel's activities when the concept seems obscure, Burgess returns to the point originated in Ennis's characterization—the need of the antiheroic personality to vindicate itself. The references to religious commitment, the death wish addressed to an unheeding God, and the momentary feelings of guilt confuse to a certain degree the antiheroic projection. The fact that Mudd, Lydgate's superior, and Lydgate's two wives seem to take greater advantage of him than he does of them also confuses the issue. But in this novel Lydgate calls upon the gangster-God for justice when he wishes for Mudd's death—he has a vision of Mudd's shrunken head and then one of his own punishment. At the novel's end, Lydgate learns that Wajak, his native mistress, is returning to the city from the interior carrying with her a special gift which can only be Mudd's shrunken head.

The eccentric plotting of *Devil of a State,* then, becomes a device to indicate to the reader the general scheme of things: because of original sin or endemic evil, there seems to be very little good in the "black" comic world of Dunia. In this novel, the anatomy of the antihero becomes clearer: his appeal to the forces of darkness is made explicit; and the appeal itself, paradoxically, suggests order and pattern and coherence, although mad. Treachery to another code becomes a consideration secondary to that of commitment to darkness. The occasional vestigial twinge of conscience becomes something very like superstition. The antihero acknowledges and appeases, just as the good Christian knocks on wood and throws salt over his shoulder.

The action of the novel is set in the caliphate of Dunia, modeled on Brunei, the uranium-rich northwestern area of Borneo bordering Sarawak (In *The Novel Now* Burgess says that Dunia was designed as "a kind of fantasticated Zanzibar" (212).). The three major plots manipulated simultaneously in *Devil of a State* are farcical in their outlines. The first, and most important of the three, concerns Frank Lydgate, fifty, twice married, temporarily separated from his Potok mistress Wajak who has gone upriver to bear a child that is not his. Lydgate, who works in the state of Dunia as European passport officer, is aware of the suffocating influence of the interior on the life of the capital: "Indeed, masts stood high above the Customs House. But there was no heartening smell of the sea here; the river sang and stenched of inland, spoke of being lost in the river-web of the colossal continent..." (7).

As the novel begins, Lydgate is searching frantically for the key to the squalid house that has been allocated to him by his superior, Mudd, who is chairman of the housing board. Lydgate knows that Mudd punishes him not so much for having a native mistress and brown children but for having witnessed Mudd's whipping of a Creole jockey in a horse race in Shurga: "That's at the back of everything. Just because we nearly had you warned off the course. And you have the damned cheek to talk about responsibilities and ideals and morality and Christ knows what" (211). Mudd points out to Lydgate that filth and dirt are Lydgate's natural element, and he also informs him that Lydia, Lydgate's second wife who has refused to divorce him, is soon to arrive in Dunia.

The second plot concerns the Tascas, father and son, who are marble workers engaged to decorate the caliph's new mosque with marble facings. They are involved in a bitter hate relationship that sustains and inspires them to violence of a peculiarly Senecan nature. Burgess wryly describes Paolo in terms of Christ: "Why, he wondered, had he been forsaken? In horizontal crucifixion he lay on the dirty bed-sheet, beard getting longer. Why had these workmen, his disciples, not brought him food, not come to comfort him with dulcet words and threats of new

strikes?" (222). Starved by his father, first contracted to certain
death on a banana plantation, then into a loveless marriage
because the terms are better, Paolo Tasca becomes the champion
of the working classes. To escape his father, he takes refuge
in the minaret of the mosque, "emulating Simon Stylites to shame
the white men in granting immediate independence to Dunia"
(244). He returns to Italy and to the arranged marriage, little
knowing that he leaves behind him his mark on Moslem Africa:
"missionary pictures of the Prophet Jesus would rouse a memory,
a recognition. And Italy...would mean freedom" (269).

The third plot develops the theme of marital responsibility
as it centers on the relationship of the Australian road engineer
Forbes of Marmion and his Chadi wife, Eileen. Eileen herself
is in love with Maximilian Hup, a civil servant leaving for Aden:
"Love, so little known on this continent, had given this woman
a soul, a capacity for choice" (125). Several subplots are manipulated at the same time and contribute to the main activities:
the ever-widening wave-lengths extend to the interior; rumors
of headhunting and cannibalism persist, and reverberations are
felt in the city.

Lydgate, the Tascas, and the Forbeses all live in the same
area of squalid houses; and they are brought together irresistibly:
Nando Tasca forgets his watch; the starving Paolo finds it and
sells it. It is purchased by Eileen for Maximilian; they are
discovered together in the rest room of the Dunia hotel by
Nando Tasca. Paolo comes upon the scene; and the various
complications are revealed. The watch is returned to Nando.
Lydgate encounters the crying Eileen, comforts her as best he
can, urges several whiskies on her, takes her home. But, since
she is too drunk to return to her husband, Lydgate takes her
into his own house and offers her water. But Forbes, having
borrowed space in Lydgate's refrigerator, has replaced Lydgate's
gin bottle full of water with a gin bottle full of gin. Eileen
drinks and soon Paolo meets her and takes advantage of "the
poor innocent little kiddy drunk of gin" (134). Lydgate follows
Forbes of Marmion to search for Eileen, "impelled...by guilt,
but by a guilt older than anything Forbes could possibly suspect" (134). All of these characters allow Burgess to transcribe,
with something like celestial happiness, many dialects, idioms,
and language patterns—sometimes to the supreme discomfort of
the reader.

The United Nations adviser, Tomlin, carries on a running dialogue with the chain-smoking caliph. He recognizes that if the Dunians, whom the Nationalist Patou supposedly represents, want a democracy, then a caliph is an anachronism. The whites, he knows, are on their way out; and the caliph has warned the United Nations not to meddle in matters of religion or state government. When the Tascas prove to be too troublesome, the caliph asks Tomlin to send them back to Tripoli; but Tomlin points out that no other marble cutters are available to complete the decoration of the mosque by the caliph's birthday. The caliph, who has ruled that no one can remain in the state without sponsorship, decides to sponsor the Tascas himself, when Tomlin refuses to continue U.N. support of them: "Both men sat back, a new image dancing between them, under the fan: two ragged infidels, drunk or immoral, certainly irresponsible, tucked under the mothering wings of an Islamic potentate" (149). Rowlandson, an Englishman with "mid-term nerves," assigned to teach football and emotional stability "to a people half devil and half child," literally loses his head to the cannibals, a fact which causes the U.N. adviser to lose his figuratively to the caliph:

You're only able to indulge in your beautiful Islamic dream because we do the dirty work. Who found uranium? Was it you? No, it was a handful of engineers and geologists, men with adequate salaries but never destined to become millionaires. . . . And, while you become rich and your lazy Chosen People watch the coconuts fall, people like me and young Rowlandson, poor young Rowlandson, try to give you government, try to show you how to build a modern state, damn it, even try to show you how to build a mosque. Young Rowlandson's dead, and he hasn't even died for an ideal which you, some day, may grow to appreciate. You've no interest in the aborigines of this State. You're a pirate king, ruling retired pirates, intruders just as much as we are. . . . Think about poor underpaid officials like Rowlandson, his head lopped off, his body eaten, in an up-river village. (231-32)

"You can tell everybody that you have to leave at once because you're ill," retaliates the caliph (232).

Sebastian Hup works as secretary to the United Nations adviser and sells confidential information to the highest bidder, whether it be Carruthers Chung, who invites Lydgate to a "blidge" party that turns out to be a "pray" rather than "play" party—the two words are the same to Chung; or to the Nationalist

leader Patou, who buys several sheets of official stationery with
bona fide "stamped" signatures on them. Bastions, an organizer,
has been refused entry into Dunia by the U.N. adviser; Patou
arranges for the organizer to enter the country "legally," over
Tomlin's paid-for signature. Caught in the transaction by the
innocuous representative of the International Herbal Health
Association, Patou pretends to be the U.N. adviser and sends
the herbalist upriver; soon it is reported that the health faddist
has lost his head to the cannibals. This report presently brings
upon the scene the first Mrs. Lydgate, also associated with the
International Herbal Health Association, to add to the dizzying
plot patterns.

The major plots are brought to a single climax in the political
rally that occurs in the Chin Chin Cinema, the local motion-
picture house. Lydgate sees Lydia in the fracas that takes place
at the Chin Chin during the political rally at which Bastions
speaks, and he soon decides to return to her. Paolo finds himself
unaccountably a champion of the working classes. Eileen decides
to continue working at her old profession. The ape who carries
Lydgate's photograph takes off his workman's coveralls in the
excitement, but he has difficulty putting them on again when
the free-for-all ends; polecats walk the theater rafters. Everyone
begins to look forward to the caliph's birthday celebrations and
to the official opening of the mosque.

The "blidge" party, to which Carruthers Chung earlier in
the narrative had invited Lydgate, had turned out to be a
religious get-together of a confessional type. Asked to confess
his sins, Lydgate had refused. But to Lydia and Mudd, Lydgate
does confess, after a party at the Chin Chin Cinema in the
caliph's honor; he admits that perhaps Carruthers Chung had
the right idea about confession easing the soul. Lydgate confesses to Mudd and Lydia that he had married the first time
for money; that, finding the marriage impossible, he had run
away from it. Dogged by his elderly wife Agnes, he had kept
running until he heard from an acquaintance that she lay
dying. Assuming her dead—"she'd no stamina, living off grass
and dandelion leaves"—he had married Lydia, only to discover
several months later that Agnes had not died (215). Abandoning
Lydia, he had gone from job to job, always encountering
superiors like Mudd. In Dunia, he had been faithful to his
Potok mistress simply because she had made no claims upon

him. He had achieved some sense of responsibility because responsibility had not been asked of him. As he confesses to Mudd and Lydia, Lydgate admits that he has felt for a long time that people had been fighting to save his soul; and he wonders if God knows why.

In the course of the narrative, Burgess introduces several passages of heightened prose that are intended to serve a religious expediency. The dreamlike quality of these passages, coupled with the religious quality of the imagery—rain that does not cleanse, justice that does not consider humanity— indicate an inner reading for the comic action; they serve as countertensions for the "comic-black" extravaganzas that both delight and disgust the reader. During one of these passages, Lydgate apostrophizes himself, thereby isolating the subterranean intention of the book. And it becomes clear to the reader that the contrived, melodramatic, farcical, undeniably hilarious activities of the plot are used simply as devices to indicate how difficult it is to achieve human understanding:

Ah, Francis Burroughs Lydgate, at it again? Hast thou in that wasted frame not one ounce, not one teaspoonful of human tenderness, not one drip off the spout of an oilcan of human tenderness? Dost thou disdain to carry on thy back the burden that all but thee accept gladly, knowing it to be the inheritance of all mankind? Not sin only, but the knowledge that taking involveth giving, that we are all members of one another, that the perfect round of man and woman in hardly contrived harmony is a shadow or figure of that heavenly round or harmony in which we are destined ultimately to merge our shrieking self-hood, becoming one with the one with the one with the
    Shut up, shut up, shut up (189)

As he attempts to leave Dunia on the day after the caliph's celebration, Lydgate discovers that he has lost his place on the plane to Paolo Tasca, who is returning to Italy to embark on a marital venture that echoes in a grotesque and comic fashion Lydgate's own first marital fiasco. The delay introduces Agnes into Dunia and returns Lydgate to her religious and fanatic authority, perhaps the worst horror of all and his punishment— hence the reference to I Corinthians. The novel ends with the caliph and his entourage looking for the key to the mosque. The rain cracks, hurls, and vomits like a sick heaven over the

mosque and the black kingdom, "heedless of human time or
of any time but its own" (282).

The headshrinkers (who shrink a Belgian's head, put the
glasses back on it and Brylcreem in the hair—"a little dab will
do you") become the means of symbolizing what Conrad called
"the heart of darkness." The upriver aspect of the symbolism
suggests the rendering of *Time for a Tiger,* but in it Crabbe
and Fenella had moved only to the perimeter of the area of
darkness. The symbolism in both novels, appropriately, suggests
much more than it states; for the question of universal guilt
is a matter of greatest importance to *Devil of a State,* and
Burgess uses symbolical means of rendering his intention. The
city of Dunia with its "half-built temples to Commerce, to
Transatlantic Cinema, to the Broadcast Word, to Allah," suggests a city of dreadful night (6). The public clock, where the
two main streets cross, symbolically has thrown up its hands
in despair at the many cuts in the electric power system: "It
was now always midday or midnight, and that seemed somehow
right for a state where there were no half-measures. Kill or be
killed, eat or be eaten; high noon or the hour of ghosts and
robbers" (39). When the thunder roars and the rain vomits
over the locked house of God, the religious meaning of the novel
becomes clear, despite the darkened sky.

The full impact of the elaborate plot and Lydgate's attempts
to come to terms with women, who worry him because they
want to be people, suddenly focus, through the responsibilities
involved in the marriage contract, on the need for understanding.
There is no preaching; whatever morality there is, the reader
himself grasps it between spasms of horror and feelings of
guilt. The sacrifice of Rowlandson to the forces of darkness
("Don't send me back there, please. There's going to be trouble,
honest there is") suggests not only the guilt of the United
Nations adviser, who had insisted that Rowlandson return to
his post because it is the duty of the English to be uncomfortable,
but also the guilt of the caliph, who is constantly supplied with
a tin of cigarettes and two ash trays (227). The Nationalists, "in
Nazi jack boots, dirty shirts, on bicycles, crinkly hair long uncut,
wild beards long unshaven," further suggest the realm of fear
and violence (5).

The light of goodness seems as erratic as the electric power
which arbitrarily fails and plunges the world of Dunia into

darkness. Taxi drivers count cars, lights, decorations, anything, suggesting the idea of a mechanical universe. The one force that seems to be at all operative is that of Love, and that force is handled darkly. The reader sees Eileen planning to return to Maximilian Hup when the ship that is ostensibly taking her and her children to her husband's Australia docks at Aden. And Lydgate at the end, getting perhaps worse than he deserves, falls into the hands of his legal wife, the fanatic herbalist-Christian Agnes, whose name means "lamb of God."

CHAPTER 5

England, Education, and the Future

I The Worm and the Ring

PUBLISHED in 1961, *The Worm and the Ring*[1] differs in several ways from the novels preceding it. It is, first of all, set in England, in 1951, during Festival of Britain time; and, except for a brief and comic foray into Paris, the action occurs in an English rural setting, a coeducational grammar school.[2] Second, the novel is not so much characterized by the "bitter fun" of *The Right to an Answer* and *Devil of a State* as by a cold irony that is immediately suggested by the epigraph from Plato's *Apologia*: "condemned on the charges of corrupting youth and substituting false gods for the gods of the borough." The forces that make it impossible for men of humane vision to live decent lives within the precincts of an institution supposedly dedicated to learning and truth are examined with intelligence, but an intelligence mixed with compassion and wit. Poor salaries, uninterested students, gossiping and malicious intruders, stupid bureaucrats who "govern" school administrations—all aspects of academic life are served a full measure of well-aimed satire.

The Worm and the Ring exhibits the attempt of the author to deal more realistically with the materials that he had before dealt with in grotesque and comic terms; the world of the novel is a corrupt, opportunistic, career-minded world in which all goes rewarded—except true merit. And in keeping with this attempt to handle materials more realistically, Burgess delineates his major characters in a more conventional manner. The plot develops gradually and moves inevitably to a predictable outcome.

Yet there is humor in the book that is both full and satisfying; and it is accomplished, in part, through the antics of the schoolchildren, notably Rich, Gilpin, and Cowie. Humor is further achieved with the parody of Wagner's *Das Rheingold* that opens

the novel and lends a mock-epic quality to the power struggle
within the school. The bottom of the Rhine River is suggested
by the rain and by the references to urinals and to the Thames.
Alberich becomes Albert Rich, Weglinda and Flosshilda, Linda
Hardy and her chum Flossie; but Hilda Connor, a voluptuous
teacher in the school, also slyly suggests Flosshilda. Linda's
adolescent diary becomes the rheingold; Wotan, Woolton, the
headmaster; and the castle of Walhalla, a shining new school
building. Fricka, Wotan's wife, becomes Frederica, affectionately
called "Frick" by her husband; and Freia, the goddess of youth
and beauty who is threatened by the giants Fasolt, Fafner, and
Froh, is the terrified Miss Fry. Loge, Wotan's adviser, is changed
into the kindly master Mr. Lodge who, in his increasing senility,
reads the tales about Gulliver and Long John Silver. The one
who finally captures the magic ring and forfeits the love of
mankind is Gardner. The Worm of the title then is the boy
Albert Rich—in the opera, Alberich transforms himself into a
great snake; and the ring is the confusion forged by the incorrigible boy. But, on a religious level, the worm and the ring
symbolize meaningful abstract qualities.

The Worm and the Ring is similar to the novels that precede
it in that it continues the appraisal of the antiheroic personality.
In this novel, the antihero is stripped of Byronic associations;
he is neither rebel nor social outcast. He is, instead, a successful
member of the academic community who is admired by the
stupid and by the mediocre but despised by Howarth and
Woolton, the novel's principal characters, who have the intelligence to see behind the mask and to understand the full horror
of the reality. In the course of the action, idealism and truth are
defeated by slander, hypocrisy, and corruption. The play for
power within the school directs the action and sets the theme,
which is quite simply that the world belongs to the deceivers,
the slanderers, and the opportunists.

In the Epilogue, the reader becomes aware that Gardner, the
successful, the glamorous, has succeeded in replacing Woolton
as headmaster because he coldly played a game of deceit and
treachery to achieve his objective. The world of Mr. Woolton's
school becomes, as was Crabbe's school in Kuala Hantu, a
microcosm of the world of men and affairs—one in which success
is the measure of greatness, not the means by which it is
achieved. Gardner is immediately recognizable as the Machiavel-

lian antihero, and his kinship to such antiheroes as Joe Lampton
of *Room at the Top* is established. There is none of the Spindrift
or the Raj about him, and little of the Lydgate. Howarth too
is antiheroic, but he is cut along more romantic lines. Albert
Rich sets the plot in motion; Gardner profits from the intrigue;
and Howarth suffers.

The Worm and the Ring also brings into open consideration
the problem of Roman Catholic allegiances in a predominantly
Protestant country. Through Christopher Howarth, whose family
lists among its Catholic ancestors an Elizabethan martyr who
pinned a copy of the pope's bull of excommunication of the
queen to the door of his Lancashire church, the social as well
as marital problems of the English Catholic are discussed (105).
Howarth, though not a practicing Catholic, although he does
say several times in the course of the novel that he intends to
make his Easter duty, is fully aware of his anomalous position;
for his wife Veronica is devoutly Roman Catholic, and their
son Peter is being reared as a Catholic. Concerning the position
of the English Catholic, Burgess observes in an essay on the
politics of Graham Greene, published in *The New York Times
Book Review*:

Deeper than party politics lies the whole question of national allegiance. The British State tolerates the Roman Catholic Church, but
the Roman Catholic Church, being a supranational body, has no
representation in the Establishment: there are no Roman Catholic
Bishops in the House of Lords, though it was found possible to put
the Methodist minister Donald Soper there. To honor the monarch
is to acknowledge the hegemony of the Church of England. Catholic
patriotism must necessarily be of a qualified kind, since not only
is the present involved but also the past, the remembered wrongs
of history. These latter are, to the really embittered, incarnated or
lapidified in the cathedrals and churches which, once Catholic, are
now Protestant.[3]

In *The Worm and the Ring* young Peter Howarth is taunted
by his schoolmates to retrieve a ball that has lodged on the roof
of the school building. "Go on, 'Owarth. England's watching
'yer," torments Rich, the boy responsible for much of the evil
in the school. Peter, whose namesake had been hanged, is
likened to "a spread-eagled frog" as he climbs toward the ball.
When the drain pipe fails to hold him—after he has sent the
ball down, however—he offers up "what was coming now for

his father, that part of his father in himself" (236-37). Christopher, who should have been supervising the children's games, has instead been seducing Hilda Connor in the juvenile library.

The marital problems relative to a Roman Catholic marriage, sex and its purpose, are elaborated upon in this novel; and ironically at the end, once Veronica has undergone a hysterectomy, the problem appears to be no longer serious. Even more ironically, Veronica seems less determined to impose Catholic doctrine on either her husband or her son after the operation. Forced to leave England to take a job selling wine in Italy and on the Continent, Christopher and his family, heading toward Rome, think more about leaving England than of drawing closer to their "spiritual" homeland.

Aware of the historical claims of religion and philosophy, Howarth attempts in his teaching to remain objective and impartial. For example, he admires Luther for his courage and conviction. Much better informed about the history of his church than Canon Moon, the Catholic spiritual adviser, Howarth appreciates the eternal struggle of good and evil in terms of the various heresies that the Church has withstood. Peter remembers one of his father's discussions with Canon Moon and secretly admires his father's superior intellect: "His father knew a lot. He remembered hearing him (himself with an ear to the door) arguing with Canon Moon, the argument about the Manichees, and Canon Moon not knowing much about it. Peter had been struck by the image of the tremendous fight going on between God and the Devil which, his father had said, were not really God and the Devil, but A and B or X and Y or Black and White. You had to choose your side, said the Manichees. Somebody would win, but you didn't know who" (209). Christopher Howarth is forced to join the battle in the school, and he sides with Woolton against Gardner, with light against darkness.

Woolton, fiftyish, burdened both with a wife going through a difficult menopause and a dying, senile mother, maintains the belief that children are good and that education is worthwhile. He is threatened by anonymous letters, by a meddling and scandal-mongering secretary, and by Gardner who covets his position. The activities of the novel are set in motion by the incorrigible Rich who steals Linda Hardy's diary, in which she has described adolescent sex fantasies which center upon Woolton. When the book falls into Gardner's hands, he spreads the information about and sees that it reaches the school authorities. But it is not so much the diary and its fictions that bring about Woolton's exit from the school as it is Howarth's indiscretions with Hilda Connor in Paris and his dereliction of duty during his son's escapade on the roof. Woolton's inheritance from his mother makes it possible for him to resign his position in the school and to plan a small private school where the emphasis will be on Classical literature, a school in which, like Candide, he will be able to cultivate his small garden.

In rescuing Linda's diary from Gardner, Howarth learns that Gardner has plagiarized word for word his, Christopher's, study of the Augustan period to "earn" his doctorate. As Howarth rescues Linda's diary he notes, surprised, that Gardner is unconcerned; he recognizes that Gardner is furiously shredding typescript which of course is the incriminating evidence, Howarth's thesis. Despite his knowledge of Gardner's criminal action in plagiarizing his manuscript and in forcing Woolton's exit from the school, Howarth in "an alcohol-shaft of intuition" realizes that all Gardner's activities have been correct:

He saw that power was right for some men as servility and failure were right for others, and that such men could perhaps justify the baseness and treachery of the means through which they obtained power by their obvious fitness for rule. He knew that, theologically and ethically, this was all nonsense, but he also knew that the School would flourish, that discipline would be maintained, and that masters on duty would perform their duty efficiently. . . . Could a man deliberately damn himself, consciously break every ethical precept, so that he could eventually work good? He had never thought about it before and henceforth it was to worry him. It was a subversion of so much he had believed. (259-60)

Thinking over his conclusions concerning the victory of the evil and the vicious, Howarth at first thinks that he will join the enemy camp. Drunk in the pub, he considers the place of "religion" in the world, and he spits on the word. He thinks that the one country he would like to visit is America, not so much for the country itself, but America as the abstraction that an army acquaintance, Captain Muller, had spoken of to him in Paris. America, Muller had said, had lost blood so fast that it had become an idea only, two-dimensional, "and everything deepfrozen" (175). "You know the legend of Theseus and the

Minotaur?" Howarth had countered; "I always think of Theseus
as the American superman...tough and clean and football
playing. The Minotaur is original sin. The Labyrinth is civil-
isation. If you kill the Minotaur the Labyrinth falls down"
(175-76).

But, as the beer warms Howarth and as the minute hand
steals toward the closing hour, he reconsiders a future based
upon his past. What sustains him, and he comes to appreciate it,
is the subterranean belief that there is goodness somewhere
in the world: "There would be wine and love and the self-
renewing cycle. And, above all, God and the various swordsharp
manifestations of God. For, despite death and toothache and
the young men tossing on their frustrated beds, the silly man
with the gun and the short-necked men brooding over maps,
the sour morning mouth and the agony of the martyrs, the
crumble of towers and town walls, life had to be blessed and
praised" (266).

The ring that the title describes is not only Wagner's, but the
ring of marriage and the ring of the horizon, both testifying
to the unity of creation and the power of God. Man's evil portion, the "worm crawling through the greening earth," becomes
itself a testimony of the existence of its opposite.

The Worm and the Ring, then, places Burgess alongside
Graham Greene and Evelyn Waugh, who both deal with the
problem of religious commitment in a fear-ridden world. Gardner
is successful, empirically; but there appears to be more to
existence than superficial order and efficiently run machinery.

However, it is Gardner who is pragmatically successful, Gardner who has used both Woolton and Howarth; Gardner who
is "Top-dog or "God-pot." Knowing that state education would
shortly replace public education, Gardner had connived to
secure the eminence that he had in fact achieved. "The change-
over will be effected very easily," says Gardner to his assembled
staff in the new building. "Three buildings, of which only this
is at present in use, face a common campus. They will, when
the scheme comes into operation, be, not three schools, but
three teaching blocks.... A unity will be made out of a trinity"
(269). And Gardner adds that the group could use Howarth
to help develop the theological image. Ennis—from *A Vision of
Battlements,* Burgess's first novel—is a music master in Woolton's
school and is mentioned several times in *The Worm and the*

Ring. Enigmatically, he asks Gardner to leave Howarth out of the discussion; for Howarth is "selling real wine" (269).

The ultimate irony is that Gardner does not care at all about education. He knows that he was born to rule, and he knows that power cannot corrupt him. Only the good, the idealistic, and the optimistic are capable of being corrupted; and there is very little in Gardner to corrupt: "Good and bad, he recognized, were terms to which he could attach no ethical significance. An action was justifiable if it led to the possession of the thing it was desirable to have. Happiness was neither here nor there: what counted in life was the fulfillment of one's own peculiar daemon, the realisation of a pattern which existed outside the caprices of appetite, ambition, desire. The man born to rule was neither the good man nor the bad, but the man capable of existing as a sheer function, a sheer personification of order" (272). To Gardner, Woolton, caught up in his dream of a Classical utopia, had, despite his liberalism, proven fundamentally irresponsible as had Howarth; they were men to be used and then set aside.

In the novels preceding *The Worm and the Ring,* the religious elements had been implied subterraneously or approached obliquely. In this novel, Burgess squarely attacks the problem of good and evil. Original sin, man's evil heritage; Manichaeanism; Augustinianism; Pelagianism; fascism; and the relative aspects of ethical behavior are investigated. More forthrightly than before, Burgess stresses the function of religion in life. The worm, significantly placed first in the title, is identified as part of life. And man, veering between good and evil, discovers his identity as he responsibly commits himself to light or darkness.

"English Catholics," Burgess says in the essay on Greene already mentioned, "are tempted by more heresies than are the children of Mediterranean baroque Christianity" (34). In England, the greatest temptation is offered by Pelagius who denied original sin and doubted that divine grace was necessary for salvation. Pelagius's doctrines, insisting on the major political ideologies of England, are most conspicuously felt in socialism: "once a Catholic lays open his soul to the corruptions of the great world of commitment, he must accept a kind of empiricism, if he is not to be damned, drawing from the natural order what may conceivably further the terrestrial ends of the supernatural order" (32).

More realistic than its predecessors, despite the brilliant par·

ody of the opening chapter, *The Worm and the Ring* develops the action primarily through the points of view of Howarth and Woolton. Gardner's "philosophical" rationalizations are necessarily placed in the Epilogue that follows Woolton's memorable resignation speech and the Howarths' departure for the Continent. Contrasting with the coldly ironical tone that the novel succeeds in maintaining are scenes warmly and comically memorable: Rich and Cowie being rescued from perverts by a drunken Howarth in a Paris bistro; Howarth seducing Hilda Connor while children throw food about in the lunchroom; Woolton attending to his dying mother as she talks constantly about fish; Lodge interviewing Linda Hardy; and Hilda Connor chastising Howarth for being a Catholic.

Since Burgess deals directly with his religious theme, there is less need in *The Worm and the Ring* for him to imply by means of imagery and symbol the hidden significance of the novel. Still, the action culminates around Eastertime, enhancing the affirmation that Howarth achieves at the novel's end, reminding the reader of the rainbow at the end of *Das Rheingold*. The references to fish and fish pie suggest slyly a Christian dimension—as does the name Veronica, for Christopher's wife turns to him a constant face of suffering. Less dazzlingly Joycean than its predecessors, perhaps because of its insularity, the novel is still a superb fiction. The dialogue, sure and easy; the cadences of the pub-drinkers' speeches right and quick; the occasional grotesque surprise—the one-eyed homosexual farmer—all demonstrate the fact that Burgess can write the more conventional kind of novel—and do so very well indeed.

II A Clockwork Orange *and* The Wanting Seed

In a chapter entitled "Utopias and Dystopias" in *The Novel Now*, Anthony Burgess appraises the influence of H. G. Wells on the modern utopian novel:

Many novelists set themselves the task—before and after the war—of exposing Wells's optimistic scientific liberalism as a sham. Science and education, said Wells, would outlaw war, poverty, squalor. All of us carry an image of the Wellsian future—rational buildings of steel and glass, rational tunics, clean air, a diet of scientifically balanced vitamin-capsules, clean trips to the moon, perpetual world peace. It was a fine dream, and what nation could better realise

it than the Germans? After all, their scientific and educational achieve-
ments seemed to put them in the vanguard of Utopia-builders. What,
though, did they give to the world? A new dark age, a decade
of misery.[4]

After dreaming of a new race, Wells, as Burgess points out,
died a disappointed liberal.

In 1962 Burgess himself published two "dystopian" novels,
A Clockwork Orange[5] and *The Wanting Seed*,[6] both conceived
and executed from the same philosophical orientation but quite
different in content and development. Both are in many ways
reminiscent of Aldous Huxley's and George Orwell's utopian
novels, but both are, more importantly, advancements of the
utopian genre and highly representative of the ideas and patterns
that inform the majority of Burgess's works. *A Clockwork Orange*,
written in the first half of 1961, is set in the near-future and,
in many ways, borrows from Orwell's *1984*; *The Wanting Seed*,
written between August and October, 1960, more elaborate and
less polemical, is set in a further-distanced future and reminds
the reader of *1984*, Huxley's *Brave New World*, Golding's *Lord
of the Flies*, and Rex Warner's *The Wild Goose Chase* and *The
Aerodrome*.

In terms of the loosely applied criteria of "black comedy,"
discussed earlier, Anthony Burgess's *A Clockwork Orange* concerns itself with a religious problem: the nature of human will
and the importance of individual choice in a socialized and
dehumanized world. A drunken prison chaplain says to Alex,
the fifteen-year-old protagonist, before he is subjected to the
Ludovico process which will force him to choose good at all
times: "It may not be nice to be good, little 6655321. It may
be horrible to be good. And when I say that to you I realise
how self-contradictory that sounds. I know that I shall have
many sleepless nights about this. What does God want? Does
God want goodness or the choice of goodness? Is a man who
chooses the bad perhaps in some way better than the man
who has the good imposed upon him. Deep and hard questions . . ." (96).

Alex, the leader of a hoodlum gang and precocious in the ways
of evil, can nevertheless appreciate the nature of the choice
he makes for evil over good. Together with Georgie, Dim, and
Pete, his "droogs," Alex's activities incorporate beatings, rob-

beries, gang wars, rape, and finally murder. Betrayed by his gang after he has forced his way into the home of an old woman who cares for scores of cats and has killed her, Alex is placed in a progressive prison where his education in evil is advanced. His "brainwashing" and his subsequent return to society form the basic plot of the novel and afford Burgess the opportunity to comment hilariously and bitterly about the condition of man in a mechanized world.

Peculiar to the gangs that invade the London nights in the socialized state that Burgess fashions is the use of Nadsat (perhaps an anagram of "satan'd," for Burgess, like Joyce, is fond of puns and whimsies), which is described as "the language of the tribe" (115): "odd bits of rhyming slang. . . . A bit of gypsy talk, too. But most of the roots are Slav. Propaganda. Subliminal penetration" (115). A combination of Russian words and descriptive phrases, odd Cockney expressions, biblical locutions, and schoolboy humor talk, all of which suggest ironic overtones, Nadsat at first appears to the reader as a barrier to communication; but it actually becomes a device that enhances the narrative. The activities of Alex and his "droogs" become more terrifying, while, ironically, the language becomes more poetical. Phrases like "Being sore athirst, my brothers," "They know not what they do or say" (9), and "mom gave me a tired little smech, to thee fruit of my womb my only son sort of" (48), by their very incongruity with the activities being described, lend a note of poetic intensity to the narrative that contrasts with the nightmare horror of the action.

When Alex and his "droogs" speak Nadsat, the reader finds himself carried to the meaning by the very cadences of the words; and shortly he is conversant not only with the denotative meaning of the words but also with the witty, ironic connotations they convey. Conversely, when Alex speaks the conventional idiom, which he must do from time to time, his cadences are flat and unconvincing. By the end of the first chapter of the novel, the reader is intrigued by the language; and he is as conversant before long with Nadsat as Alex's "droogs" are. Burgess does not hesitate to play wittily with words as often as possible to suit his purpose. One needs to look only at such words as "lewdies" for people, "dama" for woman, "malchick" for boy, "horrorshow" for good, "slovo" for word, "Bog" for God, "bezoomy" for mad to appreciate the variety as well as

the possibilities of Nadsat. What at first seems a device that
calls more attention to itself than to the development of the
novel's theme appears, upon reflection, more correctly a means
to render the action more meaningful as it emphasizes the characterization and maintains the illusion of a dehumanized world
at the same time.

Alex's world is not one of Roman Catholic good and evil, as
is Graham Greene's Brighton. Yet there are both good and evil
in Alex's cosmos, and freedom to choose evil over good becomes
the chief consideration of the book. In Alex's words: "If lewdies
are good that's because they like it, and I wouldn't ever interfere
with their pleasures, and so of the other shop. More, badness is
of the self, the one, the you or me on our oddy knockies, and
that self is made by old Bog or God and is his great pride and
radosty. But the not-self cannot have the bad, meaning they of
the government and the judges and the schools cannot allow the
bad because they cannot allow the self. And is not our modern
history, my brothers, the story of brave malenky selves fighting
these big machines? I am serious with you, brothers, over this.
But what I do I do because I like to do" (43).

Alex's England is a socialized nightmare. People are forced
by the government to live regimented lives in blocks of regimented apartments, all the same, all without individuality: "In
the hallway was the good old municipal painting on the walls
—vecks and ptitsas very well developed, stern in the dignity of
labour, at workbench and machine with not one stitch of
platties on their well-developed plotts. But of course some of
the malchicks living in 18 A had, as was to be expected,
embellished and decorated the said big painting with handy
pencil and ballpoint, adding hair and stiff rods and dirty bal-
looning slovos out of the dignified rots of these nagoy (bare,
that is) cheenas and vecks" (35).

Alex's only salvation is music, to which he responds emotionally, ecstatically. To Alex music is "gorgeousness and gorgeosity
made flesh" (36); and his reaction to it at first appears mystical
in its intensity as well as in its implications, eliciting as it does
imagery of a religious nature. But, ironically, the music fails to
raise the spirit; for Alex can react only in a physical way to the
sounds of the orchestra. For Alex, a creation of the society in
which he lives, there are no such things as love, affection, or
duty; for only mechanical sex, compliance with the strong, and

a display of power mean anything. In other words, Alex is the "clockwork orange" of the title: he is produced by a system, and he exemplifies in his actions the implications of it. He is punished by that same system when his individuality, his love of music, can no longer be ignored by it. Alex is separated from the community not for his evil but because his individuality threatens the status quo. The references to music are introduced to lend a comic as well as ironic perspective to the theme and to afford a unifying factor to the book.

Although Alex's taste in music seems eclectic—he admires modern composers (whose names are invented by Burgess for comic effect) and classical composers as well—it is Beethoven whom he most cherishes, and the *Ninth Symphony* is his favorite composition: "Then I pulled the lovely Ninth out of its sleeve, so that Ludwig Van was not nagoy too, and I set the needle hissing on to the last movement, which was all bliss. There it was then, the bass strings like govoreeting away from under my bed at the rest of the orchestra, and then the male human goloss coming in and telling them all to be joyful, and the lovely blissful tune all about Joy being a glorious spark like of heaven, and then I felt the old tigers leap in me . . ." (48). Music arouses Alex sexually. At one point he goes into the street, into a record shop, picks up two little girls, gets them drunk on "moloko" (doped milk), and then rapes them, the old "in-out in-out." "Beast and hateful animal. Filthy horror," screams one of the children as she runs from Alex's room (49). His tigers no longer leaping in him, Alex falls asleep, "with the old Joy Joy Joy crashing and howling away" (49).

In the funniest scene in the novel, Alex and his "droogs" attempt to terrorize the old woman who lives with scores of cats. As he lowers himself from a window into the room, Alex finds himself amidst the cats, their milk saucers, and the terrified old woman. To save himself, Alex, as he listens to the screeching symphony of cats and the solo of the old woman, grasps a statue of Beethoven.

Soon after this scene, deserted by his "droogs," Alex finds himself in prison for having caused the death of the "ptitsa." In order to remain near to music, the only relief that Alex has in his prison routine, Alex becomes assistant to the drunken chaplain; and his chief duty is to select and play the recordings used during religious services. When Alex finds himself confronted by evil in the form of a homosexual attack, Alex and his cellmates unite to destroy the pervert; Alex is blamed for the murder.

As a defensive measure designed to check the evil that is threatening the government and causing unrest in the state, Dr. Brodsky and the minister of the interior, or "Inferior" as Alex refers to him, have devised and sanctioned a process of conditioning human responses closely modeled on Pavlov's experiments with dogs. Alex volunteers for the brainwashing process, feeling that nothing worse can happen to him; but he is mistaken. The process of conditioning, referred to as the "Ludovico process," reminds the reader, of course, of Alex's passion for old Ludwig Van himself. The rehabilitation involves the showing of atrocity films and films of violence, horror, and terror of all kinds. A drug, injected into Alex's system immediately before he witnesses the films, induces nausea; and Alex soon begs to be released from the torment of witnessing the films. His pain becomes so intense that Alex soon discovers that he will do anything to avoid it—indeed, the evil that once had given him such passionate pleasure makes him ill. To do good, even to think good, is the only remedy for the discomfort that has been built into him by the Ludovico process.

Along with the conditioning films that Alex is forced to watch and "appreciate" there are, unfortunately, musical accompaniments; and frequently the music is Beethoven's. Thus the one factor that had set Alex apart from his "droogs," Dim and Georgie and Pete, becomes for him a new measure of pain. If before Alex was a "clockwork orange," subliminally conditioned by his society, now the irony is twofold. Before his brainwashing Alex had chosen, consciously as he thought, the evil action. As a result of his reintegration into a conventionalized society by means of Ludovico processing, Alex is denied choice itself. But, not fully comprehending the extent to which his psyche has been programmed, Alex seeks after his release the ecstasy of a musical binge. Pain and nausea result. To forestall the anguish that results from any confrontation with violence or terror, Alex, who had once reveled in evil, finds himself begging and pleading for everyone's pardon; he has become one of the meek. But the earth is not his to inherit.

At this point the devices of melodrama serve Burgess well, for coincidence and chance unify the activities of the plot. Those very "lewdies" that Alex and his "droogs" had terrorized return to haunt and torment Alex in his newly discovered world of good action. A man who had been attacked while returning home with library books on crystallography sees Alex in the library where he has gone to escape the excruciating torment of piped-in music and exacts his measure of vengeance. When Alex begs for love and forgiveness, he receives instead a terrible beating. Rescued by the police, among whom is Dim, a former "droog," Alex is beaten and is left, covered with blood and half alive, in the country.

Perhaps the most obvious aspect of the melodramatic plotting concerns F. Alexander, the author of a novel entitled *A Clockwork Orange*. During an evening's escapade, Alex and his "droogs," wearing plastic masks, had forced their way into F. Alexander's house, a place significantly called "Home," where Alex had remarked the similarity of names. The gang had raped F. Alexander's wife, who had later died as a result of the outrage. It is to the house called "Home" that Alex once again finds his way. Left by the police, he finds himself befriended by F. Alexander himself. Aware of the irony, Alex for a time forestalls the author's awareness that he, Alex, now a famous personage because of his Ludovico processing, is the same Alex who had invaded the Alexander home earlier on.

Through F. Alexander, Alex is put in communication with the political party attempting to unseat the party that had determined that goodness could be forced upon people. Alex—who becomes a cause, then an issue, in the new political campaign—discovers that once again he is being used; for neither party is at all concerned with his moral emasculation. To serve party interests, Alex is programmed to commit suicide. Rather than endure the constant playing of music mysteriously coming into the locked apartment where he has been placed for his own "safety," Alex jumps from a window. "Friend," says one of the politicians who had coerced Alex, "friend, little friend, the people are on fire with indignation. You have killed those horrible villains' chances of reelection. They will go and will go for ever and ever. You have served Liberty well" (168). But Alex is aware that he has been used; he also realizes that, had he died as a result of the jump, he would have served even better the cause of political expediency.

Either as a result of Alex's fall or as a result of reverse

Ludovico processing—the point is never clarified—Alex returns to his old terror-loving, "bolshy" music ways. His final action in the American edition is to return to his "pee" and "em's" house, from which he had been dispossessed by an ersatz son, and to the music of Ludwig Van's *Ninth Symphony*: "Oh, it was gorgeosity and yumyumyum," writes Alex at the novel's end. "When it came to the Scherzo I could viddy myself very clear running and running on like very light and mysterious nogas, carving the whole litso of the creeching world with my cutthroat britva. And there was the slow movement and the last lovely singing movement still to come. I was cured all right" (174-75).

The William Heinemann 1962 edition of *A Clockwork Orange* includes a chapter wisely omitted from the American editions. The last section of the English edition emphasizes a time perspective on the activities that Alex narrates to his "brothers" in the body of the novel, by pointing out quite simply that Alex had reached the ripe old age of nineteen. His luscious glory has been sacrificed to the current fashion of shaved heads, and Alex now wears wide trousers, a black leather belt, and shiny black leather jerkins. Only the heavy boots, fine for kicking, remain. Employed by the National Grasmodic Archives "on the music side," Alex earns good money; and he cherishes a desire "to keep all my pretty polly to myself."[7] He also finds himself reluctant to participate in the horror-show activities he plans for his new gang of "droogs," preferring to listen to lieder and to study the picture of a baby "gurgling goo goo goo" which he has cut out of a newspaper. Alex is, indeed, bored; the only thoughts that interest him are of wife, son, and God. And these thoughts suggest a possible salvation for the antiheroic monster of the greater part of the novel; and the idea of possible salvation contradicts the rationale that animates the novel.

The final paragraphs of the 1962 edition attempt to reestablish the rationale but fail, for the idea of Alex as a father concerned with the future of the earth does not fulfill the characterization so brilliantly developed in the greater part of the novel: "And so it would itty on to like the end of the world, round and round and round, like some bolshy gigantic like chelloveck, like old Bog himself . . . turning and turning a vonny grahzny orange in his gigantic rookers. . . . And to all others in this story profound shooms of lip music brrrrrr. And they can kiss my sharries.

But you, O my brothers, remember sometimes thy little Alex that was. Amen. And all that cal" (196).

In the course of *A Clockwork Orange*'s activities Burgess comments in "black comic" fashion on the horror of life without choice, whether for evil or for good. It is better, he says, to choose evil rather than to be denied the right of choice. Although the direct expression of an orthodox religious code does not figure dominantly within the narrative, the point that moral action and ethical rightness are essential to life in an ordered community is cogently made. Indeed, the final impression that the novel makes is that it is a parable. The point that is left undeveloped concerns the nature of government and the nature of individual responsibility. Burgess forces his reader to come to some logical conclusion, through his "creeching horror-show" scenes, about the choice for right and good action in a civilized community. Frighteningly enough, to choose evil is a privilege that cannot be denied the individual; for, when his choice for evil has been curtailed, his choice of or for good becomes meaningless.

That Alex is as much a "clockwork orange" before as after the Ludovico treatment is ironically and comically portrayed. The sociological implications of the theme are constantly emphasized; and the reader, mystified by the manner and seduced by the virtuosity of the language, at first fails to appreciate the simple homily that man is responsible to himself and to his fellow man.

Burgess, then, in *A Clockwork Orange,* succeeds in garbing a simple thesis in a startlingly telling and darkly humorous disguise. The violence and brutality—the slashing and rapings of the hoodlum gangs, the pack-hunting, the wanton killings—all that Alex represents, all can be found described in today's newspapers. The ultimate terror that Burgess suggests, and what best represents his concern for human beings is that what Alex and his "droogs" symbolize, governments too are involved in, and that depersonalization of family and community life produces "clockwork oranges," that regimentation of human animals into mechanized and orderly units of productive enterprise produces a world without meaning, a world without hope. Symbolically, the world that Alex lives in is one devoid of light and sun; and the majority of scenes take place at night. The people that he lives among are clearly "clockwork oranges," despite the fact that they have not been submitted directly to Ludovico processing.

Like *A Clockwork Orange*, *The Wanting Seed* is set in the future, one perhaps somewhat more remote than that of *A Clockwork Orange* but one as easily realizable. Conceived from the same comic-ironic perspective, employing both fantasy and melodrama to achieve its effects, this novel confronts the immediate problem of overpopulation as it considers various possible solutions for staving off a crisis occasioned by an underproduction of foodstuffs. But the novel goes beyond the immediate implications of a hunger crisis to develop the theme of historical necessity and, indirectly, the need of mankind to accept and appreciate the ethics or morality of tested codes of behavior. Both religion and government come in for a full share of satire as Burgess moves his characters through bizarre, grotesque, and ridiculous situations.

The Wanting Seed, is, as has been noticed, also reminiscent of George Orwell's *1984* and Aldous Huxley's *Brave New World*. England in Burgess's world is a member of Enspun (The English Speaking Union), reminding the reader of Orwell's Oceania and Newspeak vocabulary. The Ministry of Infertility and the Ministry of Fertility remind the reader of the Ministry of Truth and other such designations in Orwell's book. Other similarities are the poverty that overshadows the communal life as the land refuses to yield a harvest; population police; the fear that inhibits action; food substitutes such as synthelac and cutlets of reconstructed vegetable dehydrate; a phony war; and edited news communiqués. Tristram Foxe, the protagonist of *The Wanting Seed*, is also in some way like Winston Smith of *1984*. Both are introverted, concerned with time and flux: Winston edits news releases and rewrites history; Tristram is a history teacher in a boys' school. The homsexuality encouraged by the government as a device to curtail birth and general promiscuity are exaggerations, to a degree, of Huxley's liberal morality of *Brave New World*; and the rouged, powdered, and manicured homosexual police are reminiscent of similar inventions in Rex Warner's *The Wild Goose Chase*, as are the elements of fantasy and horror which help to create the ambiance of the book.

But here similarities end, for *The Wanting Seed*, like *A Clockwork Orange*, gives evidence of Burgess's originality, his range of interests, his concern with the nature of government, and his passion for individual freedom. Exaggeration, grotesqueness, caricature, farce, and, most of all, wit distinguish the novel. Both terror and horror lend unity and allow Burgess the opportunity to exploit his themes. A heavy tone of irony at times intrudes upon the activities of the melodramatic plot, but comic and witty allusions to literature, music, language, and myth balance the horror and make the fable intellectually apt; without such comic balancing, *The Wanting Seed* would be unbearable.

Again Burgess plays dazzlingly with language as he had done in *A Clockwork Orange*: Joycean portmanteau words such as "howrashyouare," puns, and anagrams all add to the dimension of comic horror. God is referred to as "Dog"; "God knows" becomes "Dognose"; a favorite comic-strip character is "Mr. Livedog," an anagram for "Evil god"; music has gone well beyond the "conventional" stage of that in *A Clockwork Orange* and has become "concrete": "spoons rattling in tin basins, a speech made by the minister of Pisciculture, a lavatory cistern filling up, a revving engine; all recorded backwards, augmented or diminished, thoroughly mixed" (38). Cannibalism, at first revolting, becomes bearable and then even funny as men "cheerfully" band together into Dining Clubs. A gruesome logic develops from the argument that if Catholics eat the body and drink the blood of their God—it is called Eucharistic ingestion—then why can't men eat their meatier brothers to stay alive?

The Wanting Seed moves on several levels: fable, allegory, and myth. At times, the various levels of meaning uncomfortably overlap; but, on the whole, Burgess handles his materials capably. All three levels of meaning converge in the birth of Tristram's twins which occurs, symbolically, in a manger. On its simplest level of meaning, that of fable, *The Wanting Seed* moves the action from a time of infertility to a time of fertility in a future society. At the beginning of the novel, Beatrice-Joanna, married to Tristram Foxe but having an affair with his brother Derek, is shown giving the dead body of her son to the Phosphorous Reclamation Department and receiving her condolence. Constantly impatient with her kind husband, Beatrice-Joanna nevertheless wonders why she prefers Tristram's brother Derek who, to succeed in high government circles, affects homosexuality to a degree of adeptness that both amuses and terrifies her. Derek is comically pursued by Captain Loosely, a subordinate, who is attempting to discredit him with the government on the grounds that he is heterosexual. Later on, when the government condemns homosexuality and condones normal sex, Loosely, the plot manipulator, attempts to prove the opposite—that Derek, who by this time has become very important in the Ministry of Fertility, is homosexual.

Passed over for promotion, ostensibly because of heterosexuality, and told by Loosely of his wife's infidelity, Tristram finds himself accidentally involved in a street riot; he is kept imprisoned by his brother Derek, to whom he writes obscene letters. In prison, he is later told, again by Loosely, that Beatrice-Joanna is to bear a child. While on his way to Beatrice-Joanna, who has gone to her sister's North-country to bear her children, twin boys, who may have been fathered by either Tristram or Derek, or both, Tristram, hungry and cold, is tricked into the army; and he shortly finds himself involved in a war of extermination. Bewildered by the enemy, riddled by gunfire, but shielded by the dead body of a comrade, Tristram pretends death as the extermination squad approaches him to render the "old coop de gracy." He uses his platoon's money to escape from the battlefield, which is Ireland, to return to England and to restore himself to the world of the living; then he makes his way to Brighton and Beatrice-Joanna, after comically bewildering army bookkeepers by being alive and by proving that he is alive, and to a new position as a history teacher.

Burgess makes the fable appealing by the ingenuity of his episodes as well as by the virtuosity of their "black-comic" detail: Tristram's meeting with Loosely in prison, the fight with brother Ambrose over the synthechoc, his escape from imprisonment, his cheerful reception into a Diner's Club, the general bewilderment and illogicality of army life—all these scenes are brilliantly and sharply delineated, and horror and comedy are neatly balanced. As the reader watches Beatrice-Joanna turn to the sea and pray to the forces of life and vitality at the fable's end, her "gurgling wooly rosy twins" by her side, a note of hope is struck, for her a *vita nuova*. "Sea, sea," she prays; and her prayer is immediately answered, for Tristram touches her arm, she clings to him, and he becomes for her "sea, sun, tower" (223).[8]

On its simplest level of meaning, Burgess demonstrates ironically that society is capable of trading one evil for another; sanity indeed becomes a handicap when one lives in a mad world. The crucial scene of the novel is the prison scene in which Tristram suddenly discovers his animal nature, while being lectured to by Brother Ambrose, a drunken and defrocked priest. Like Graham Greene's whiskey priest, Tristram at this point becomes a pursuer, although his stay in the army temporarily interrupts his search; he discovers the proper way to live in a mad world is to be mad.

On the allegorical level, the novel becomes a means of illustrating a historical theory, both propounded and exemplified by Tristram in his role as historian. Early in the novel, where Tristram is shown lecturing his class on a cyclical theory of history, he marks off three arcs: "We have a Pelagian phase," he lectures the unheeding boys. "Then we have an intermediate phase.... This leads into an Augustinian phase.... Pelphase, Interphase, Gusphase, and so on, for ever and ever" (16). In the Pelphase, the government commits itself to the belief that man is perfectible and that, through his own efforts, he can achieve the perfection that he also desires. There is cooperation between leader and citizen; and laws are constituted as guides rather than restrictions to the ultimate end of social perfectibility: "Thus the Pelagian state does not think it necessary to erect an elaborate punitive apparatus. Disobey the law and you will be told not to do it again or fined a couple of crowns. Your failure does not spring from Original Sin" (17). In this liberal society, the state controls production but remains always subservient to the will and need of the citizen.

The dream of perfectibility is, however, destroyed by disappointment; for the leaders soon discover that men are not so good as they thought they were: "Disappointment. *Disappointment.* DISAPPOINTMENT.... The governors ... become disappointed when they find that men are not as good as they thought they were. Lapped in their dream of perfection, they are horrified when the seal is broken and they see people as they really are. It becomes necessary to try and force the citizens into goodness. The laws are reasserted, a system of enforcement of those laws is crudely and hastily knocked together. Disappointment opens up a vista of chaos. There is irrationality, there is panic. When the reason goes, the brute steps in. Brutality!" (17-18).

Uninterested in the cyclical movement occasioned by man's dual nature, Tristram's students awaken to his words only when he begins to describe the Interphase: "Beating-up. Secret Police.

Torture in brightly lighted cellars. Condemnation without trial.
Finger nails pulled out with pincers. The rack. The cold-water
treatment.... And all this because of disappointment" (18).
"What, sir, is the cold-water treatment?" asks one of his students.

Soon the Interphase gives way to the Augustinian phase, or
the Gusphase: "The orthodox view presents man as a sinful
creature from whom no good at all may be expected. A different
dream . . . a dream which, again, outstrips the reality. It eventually
appears that human social behavior is rather better than an
Augustinian pessimist has a right to expect, and so a sort of
optimism begins to emerge. And so Pelagianism is reinstated"
(21). Another boy asks, "What do they gouge out eyes with, sir?"

The Wanting Seed illustrates this cyclical theory of history.
Tristram observes the decline of the Pelphase at the novel's
beginning. The riot in the street in which Tristram is appre-
hended by the police signals the Interphase, which is soon
replaced by the lust, cannibalism, and imprisonments of the
Gusphase. Citizens are protected by the copulation police, and
excess population is destroyed by phony wars. Tinning or can-
ning of human flesh somehow makes cannibalism more tolerable
within a "civilized" world. The birth of Beatrice-Joanna's twins
signals the return of a Pelphase, and the cycle begins again.

Tristram's concern is with the historical aspects of the
Pelphase-Interphase-Gusphase cycle. He observes clinically that
the Interphase that he himself is caught up in is one of the
shortest on record, and the reader observes that the entire span
of the novel covers slightly more than the time it takes Beatrice-
Joanna to conceive and bear her children. But Beatrice-Joanna's
concern is farther reaching than Tristram's; it is with continuity.
Early in the novel, she observes a statue that crowns the government building, "the figure of a bearded man, classically robed,
glaring at the sun.... A cynosure to ships, man of the sea,
Pelagius. But Beatrice-Joanna could remember a time when it
had been Augustine. And, so it was said, he had been at other
times the King, the Prime Minister, a popular bearded guitarist,
Eliot (a long-dead singer of infertility), the Minister of Pisciculture, captain of the Hertfordshire Men's Sacred Game eleven,
and—most often and satisfactorily—the great unknown, the magi-
cal Anonymous" (15). Beatrice believes that, if there is a God,
He inhabits the sea; for the sea, to her, means life: it utters a
sound that can never be stilled. In a moment of prophetic

insight, she feels that her mission is to restore sanity and dignity to the world. In her pride, however, she identifies her mission with her Anglo-Saxon heritage; she contrasts her "English peach" with the "damson, gold, even puce" complexions of her fellow inhabitants of the British Islands, people who are predominantly Eurasian, European, and Euro-Polynesians. But the answer to her prayer comes not from the sea that she looks toward at the novel's end, but from the land, from Tristram's warm hand placed on her arm—from love. As she turns from the sea, she hears the waves break with joyful waters. The allusion is to Valéry's "Le cimetière marin."

To suggest the recurrence of the various cycles illustrated by the adventures of Beatrice-Joanna and Tristram, Burgess uses a simple yet effective device, one perhaps suggested by that old singer of infertility, T. S. Eliot himself—allusion. Tristram Foxe reminds the reader of the Tristram of Arthurian legend as well as the Tristram Shandy of Laurence Sterne's novel. The Foxe aspect of his name reminds one of crafty Reynard as well as the Foxe of the *Book of Martyrs*. The heroine's name suggests Dante's Beatrice and Thomas Middleton's Beatrice-Joanna in *The Changeling*, a creature of desperate passions, as well as Shelley's Beatrice Cenci. Derek means "leader of men," and Brother Ambrose Bayley suggests the religious order and the failure of the conventual life. There are also references to Greek and Roman as well as Christian events, each one in its way subtly emphasizing the aptness of Tristram's historical observations.

The use of allusion also allows Burgess to deal wittily with Christian myth and ritual. Tristram emerges as a questing knight moving through a ravaged land in search of the Perilous Chapel which he discovers on Easter Day, a gray anonymous building: "Never in his life had he seen an interior so large. It could not be called a room—a hall, meeting-place, place of assembly; there must be a special word and he searched for it. . . . Tristram recognized an altar on a rostrum at the far end; rows of rough benches, people sitting, waiting, kneeling, praying" (158).

Tristram suddenly realizes that the word he had been searching for is "church" and that he is in the midst of a "congregation"; and he takes a pew and listens to the "sermon": "This is Easter Day. This morning we celebrate the resurrection or rising-from-the-dead of Our Lord Jesus Christ. Crucified for preaching the

kingdom of God and brotherhood of man.... He rose to bear
witness to the world that there is no death.... He rose to extol
life everlasting, not a white-lipped ghost-life in some tenebrose
noosphere.... His blood is not only the blood of man, beast,
bird, fish; it is also the rain, the river, the sea. It is the ecstatically
pumped seed of men and is the flowing richness of the milk
of mothers of men. In Him we become one with all things,
and He is one with all things and with us" (159). The "wanting
seed" of the novel's title is identified as Love, and it is to Love
that Beatrice-Joanna prays as she confronts the sea.

Christian aspects of the novel are also elaborated in the
nativity scene, for Beatrice-Joanna gives birth to her twins in
a stable. Immediately after the nativity, the dying pig revives
and the hens begin to lay again, as they do in Bernard Shaw's
Saint Joan once de Baudricourt has decided to take the Maid
to the Dauphin. Fertility returns to the land slowly but surely,
but the reader finds it difficult to forget the eating of children,
disguised in the expression "Eucharistic ingestion." His sympathies remain with Beatrice-Joanna's brother-in-law, Shonny,
who sees Beatrice through her labor and yet loses his own
children in the slaughter of the innocents that follows. Although
hope may be implied in the mysterious birth of the twins, for
Beatrice-Joanna believes that both Tristram and Derek have
fathered her children, the horror and terror of cannibalism leave
a strong mark upon the reader's imagination.

In *A Clockwork Orange* Burgess manages to maintain a fine
equilibrium between comedy and horror. The character of his
antihero allows him to develop his theme of a depersonalized
society endangered by the unplanned-for individuality of one
of its citizens. Alex is punished as much for his uniqueness as
for his legal transgressions. Comedy balances horror; in the
midst of horror, laughter is ready to hand; and without the
laughter the fable would be intolerable. But in *The Wanting
Seed*—a much more hopeful novel than its predecessor—the
horror, leavened by wit and enriched by allusion, almost overwhelms the humor because equilibrium between the two is not
so steadily maintained. Funny though individual sequences may
be, brilliant though the plotting and the working out of the
several levels of meaning may be, precocious though the language
is, the novel fails. And this failure is unfortunate, for the symbolism of the ending seems exactly right.

CHAPTER 6

The Joseph Kell Books

ANTHONY Burgess has written two novels under the name of Joseph Kell, a pseudonym suggested by his father's first name, by the eighth-century illuminated manuscript, the *Book of Kells*, and by the *K* of Kafka. *Inside Mr. Enderby* was written first, from January to April, 1960, but was not published until 1963. *One Hand Clapping*, written between November and December, 1960, was published in 1961.[1] Both novels were written pseudonymously to "hide evidence of over-production,"[2] but each presents additional evidence of Burgess's experimentation with form; each is perhaps more than any of his other books bleak and despairing.

I   One Hand Clapping

One Hand Clapping,[3] a tour de force, is the story of a better-than-average-looking young English couple who live in industrial Bradcaster, familiar Burgess terrain. The activity of the novel is recounted in the first person by Janet Shirley, the twenty-three-year-old wife of twenty-seven-year-old Howard Shirley, a used-car salesman with a photographic memory. Janet is, to a certain extent, the product of contemporary advertising and merchandising. Barely educated, she works in a supermarket where she methodically stocks shelves with canned goods. The language of the novel is hers, and Burgess carefully and brilliantly forces it to yield the essential meaning of his piece. At times, Janet herself is aware of the implications of the story she is recounting; at others, the reader is forced to draw conclusions and decide for himself what the meaning of the parable is.

The title, *One Hand Clapping*, promises more than the novel offers—an attempt to deal with Zen Buddhism. Howard and Janet go at one point to a play in London, one that has been well reviewed by the *Times* as "a play dealing with the decay and decadence in the world about us, very witty" (128). Burgess's novel, like the play, deals with contemporary decadence. And, like the play, the novel is also intended to be "a way of getting in touch with Reality . . . proceeding by way of the absurd. . . . Like imagining thunder with no noise and a bird flying with no body or head or wings. It's supposed to be a way of getting to God" (128-29).

Although *One Hand Clapping* does use at several points the imagery of Zen Buddhism, it does not deal with the philosophical aspects of Zen. If there is a philosophical referent, which is debatable, it is more nearly contemporary Existentialism in its nihilistic emphasis; for Howard is determined to destroy himself and Janet as a protest against the mechanized, decadent world that he reads about in the *Daily Window*. The newspaper assumes symbolical proportions within the novel, for it becomes Howard's way of looking at the absurd activities of the era. A film actress's new baby (the same Rayne Waters who appears in *The Doctor Is Sick*) is given front-page coverage while the back page lists statistically the results of an airline disaster— an irony Burgess had pointed out earlier in *The Doctor Is Sick*.

The meaning of the novel is furthermore complicated by the fact that Howard is insane. His ability to remember statistics from the past and to foresee the future amounts to an abnormality, as Janet herself is aware. Howard Shirley's photographic memory equips him to deal advantageously with a television quiz show symbolically called *Over and Over*. When he chooses books as his subject and answers questions dealing with the most superficial facts of literature, he feels guilty; for he recognizes that he is in some way betraying the ideals of the past as well as the genuine scholarship of the present. He wins the thousand-pound prize, puts the money on horses, and amasses a tidy fortune of approximately eighty thousand pounds.

Howard's plan is to see whether the contemporary world is worth living in by spending his money on the best merchandise that civilization purveys. At several moments Janet becomes dimly and ironically aware of the fact that most museums are free, but not so Howard. The difficulty with the test is that Howard does not play fair: he has already decided the outcome. He says to Janet: "What I wanted to do really was to sort of prove to both of us that there wasn't all that much you could do with money and that business about living pleasant was really a load of nonsense. Because the world's a terrible place and getting worse and worse every day, and no matter how much you try to live pleasant you can't hide the fact that it's a rotten world and not worth living in" (158). Ironically he recognizes that what has allowed him to make the test is his photographic brain, "a sort of mockery, like having a machine fixed inside your skull" (159).

The point that Burgess is making is that Howard has lost identity in a world that his wife Janet leaves largely unquestioned. She is more concerned with her appearance, or with preparing beans or spaghetti on toast, than she is with the world outside her little orbit. The money that Howard wins forces her into a glossy, vulgar, and surfeiting world—she is literally sick several times on the rich food that she and Howard consume on their spending spree. The money that forces Janet out of the supermarket also brings into her orbit Redvers Glass ("Revers'd" Glass, perhaps), a poet. For Howard sends the thousand pounds he wins on the quiz program to a reporter on the *Daily Window,* who gives nine hundred of it to Glass.

Glass represents, as artists frequently do in Burgess's works, the attempt to wrest meaning from the chaos of human existence. Howard commissions Glass to write a death poem, establishing by doing so an equivocal alter-ego motif. Janet, who is also attracted to Glass, finds his physicality a refreshing relief from her husband's more gentle ways. While Janet and Howard are traveling in the United States and in the West Indies, Glass moves into their house to work on the commissioned piece. When Howard and Janet return, Glass attempts to warn Janet of Howard's morbid intentions; but she refuses to accept his warnings. Glass, as the novel continues, becomes more and more like Janet.

When it becomes apparent to Janet that Howard plans in fact to kill them both as a macabre birthday present to her, she fights with teeth of iron. She manages to defend herself with a coal-hammer, and kills Howard accidentally. Although Janet is not portrayed as admirable—she accepts things as they are—the reader's sympathies are with her at this point of the narrative, strangely, perhaps, because Howard is the more sympathetic of the two. What follows is "black comedy" of the most gruesome sort.

Janet finds Redvers Glass, induces him by bribery and threat

to help her dispose of Howard. His body is stuffed into a
pigskin trunk, shipped to Paris, eventually transferred to a
camphorwood chest, and kept constantly by Janet's side. When
Redvers soon betrays Janet for another woman—and she him—
she keeps the coal-hammer with Redver's fingerprints on it as
a threat. She relishes her power over Glass: "Because now all
Red has to do is to say he's sick of the modern world and he
wants to leave it, taking me with him, and then the old coal-
hammer will come into play, and that won't be murder, it will
be self-defence, like with Howard" (205).

The difficulty with the novel is the intentional ambiguity
that Burgess builds into it. There is neither villain nor hero in
One Hand Clapping; for Howard is insane, Janet is as much
victim as foil, and Redvers Glass becomes simply Howard's
means of immortalizing himself as he shuffles himself off from
an absurd world. Not even society appears convincingly vil-
lainous, for Burgess does little more than to define superficially,
hampered as he is by the mentality of his narrator, the aspects
of the world that befuddle Howard. Perhaps Burgess designs
an excess of reason as the culprit, yet Howard's photographic
brain suggests a limitation of reason. If the Janet who stacks
cans in the supermarket is slightly deceitful, then Howard who
reads widely understands superficially. If Howard emerges more
sympathetically than does Janet, Burgess patently does not
condemn her. She tells her story neatly, economically—there
are twenty-seven chapters, one for each year of Howard's life.

What Janet asks of life is not unreasonable. When she blames
her lack of understanding on the fact that she has received poor
training from her schoolteachers, the reader cannot fully credit
her; but the point is a cogent one. She realizes that society is
glossy, vulgar, and deceitful; but she remembers what Howard
forgets—that, though Elizabethan times were smelly and foul,
they produced Elizabeth I. Janet lives in the here and the now,
but not in the Zen Buddhist sense; for she lives without ques-
tioning, without probing, without testing the ultimate ground
of here and now. Howard's test of the here and now is obfuscated
by his determination to destroy himself. He is, furthermore,
diminished by his limited reason, his lack of intuition. To choose
death, in preference to life, simply to make a point of protest
is also far from Zen. Nihilism, perhaps Existentially determined,
is Howard's obsession.

These back and forth patterns suggest, however, that Howard and Janet are really one, with differences. The moments of telepathic communication, the genuine affection that the two share, and Janet's easy willingness to accommodate Howard's desire to give away all of "his," rather than "their," money suggest other levels of meaning in the novel but add still more to the patterns of ambiguity that the novel attempts to portray. Moreover, Janet's survival and old Pop's wartime question, "How long do you think this war's going to last, Corporal?" and the answer, "What does it matter how long it lasts so long as there's still plenty of beer and fags?" do little to offset the nihilist mood that *One Hand Clapping* creates. Janet concludes her narrative with a reference to Howard's army service: "Howard, by the way, when he was doing his national service, was said by everybody not to be much of a soldier. Let me like a soldier fall. That's just what he didn't say, did he? Poor silly Howard" (206). The reader remembers Howard's saying earlier, "The point is that somebody's got to protest against the world as it is, and we're the people who're going to do it." And Janet's reply is "Oh, nonsense" (179).

Although the various components of the novel are well integrated into Janet's narrative, *One Hand Clapping* is not completely successful. The American scenes are vaguely and disturbingly delineated; the London scenes, on the other hand, are sharply portrayed. Since Howard is determined to prove civilization meaningless, everything seems somehow prearranged. The "black comedy" of the end of the novel—the disposition of Howard's corpse—darkens even more the mood of the novel. The reader is not so much implicated in Janet's lack of guilt and responsibility as he is enchanted by her ability to deal squarely with the bother of disposing of a body.

The triumph of the novel—and no mean one—is the ability to make Janet's mind the stage of the novel's action. The method is vaguely reminiscent of Ford Madox Ford's in *The Good Soldier,* and Ford's expression, the "biography of an affair," explains, to a limited degree, Burgess's technique. Janet is to date Burgess's most fully developed female character, and his handling of her psychology is admirable. The references to the Zen Buddhist "sound" of one hand clapping, although used ironically, do little more than offer a hint of an explanation:

but they do underscore poignantly Howard's protest against
the absurdity of a meaningless existence.

II   Inside Mr. Enderby

While in Paris with Albert Rich and the other children of
the Woolton school, Christopher Howarth, in *The Worm and
the Ring*, runs into Muller, a friend from army days. In a bistro,
they recall an earlier meeting in which they had spoken of sin
and civilization, likening the minotaur of Classical legend to
original sin and the labyrinth to civilization itself. "If you kill
the Minotaur the Labyrinth falls down," the despondent Catholic
Howarth had said to his wine-merchant friend.[4]

In *Inside Mr. Enderby*,[5] Anthony Burgess deals again with
the Minotaur legend, making a similar application. Published
in 1963, *Inside Mr. Enderby* tells the story of an identity crisis,
one which involves the dissolution of a poet and his re-creation
into a "useful" member of society. Enderby, an antihero-artist,
like his much younger Joycean counterpart Stephen Dedalus,
has chosen to give up family, religion, and country in order to
serve in the temple of art. Anally obsessed, forty-five, balding,
dyspeptic, flatulent, onanistic, egotistical, shy, loving, and crafty,
Enderby is, in the early parts of the book, a true protestant:
he protests by his way of life against all the trammeling influences
of a decadent, disgusting civilization. Like the historical Luther,
or perhaps John Osborne's Luther (for both Enderby and
Osborne's play are of the same time), Enderby hates the pope,
grumbles constantly about his own stomach pains, and frequently expels the devil, a flatus, through his anus. He composes
his lyrics while seated on the toilet, illustrating comically the
relationship between the Manichaean world of corruption and
the Pelagian desire to create a perfect moment in time.

The poem that Enderby devotes the greater part of his efforts
to during the novel is a redaction of the minotaur myth, a
combination of both Cretan and Christian elements. Entitled
The Pet Beast, the poem tells of the god's visitation and of the
birth of a monster with gentle eyes that are "twin worlds of
love" (18). Minos builds a labyrinth, and the monster is hidden
within it. Harrowing stories spring up to describe the monster's
wanton and bloodthirsty ways. Soon the monster becomes the
state's guilt. One who has never known guilt, a Pelagian liberator,

comes to the labyrinth and leads the Minotaur from the maze: "Humanity seized it and reviled it and buffetted it. Finally it was nailed to a cross where it died slowly" (18). With the death of the gentle monster, the labyrinth collapses; the artifices of culture—museum and library—fall into dust; and an end comes to a cycle.

One of the technical problems that confronts Enderby as he works out the parts of his poem on his bottom-polished wooden throne is the introduction of the labyrinth-maker, the Dedalus figure, the architect or artist. As the action of the novel progresses, the reader becomes aware that Enderby is intended as both artist and victim and that he may very well be the Pelagian liberator who brings about the destruction of the monster with loving eyes.

When Rawcliffe, Enderby's alter ego within the complicated plot, and Vesta Bainbridge, the "widow in the meadow" whom Enderby fearfully causes to materialize out of his subconscious, appear, the reader recognizes the psychological complications of the myth; and the maze becomes the poet's mind. Rawcliffe comes to represent Enderby's fear of the diminishing of his lyrical gifts; Vesta, his reluctance to be involved in the banalities of everyday living. Vesta becomes Ariadne within the novel's framework, showing Enderby the way out of the maze into the world, represented by *Fem*, a woman's magazine. The name Vesta reminds the reader of Ariadne's function as priestess within a temple dedicated to the worship of a female principle. And, like Theseus, Enderby abandons his "savior," but in Rome rather than on Naxos.

Just as Enderby becomes aware of the fact that the chief interest of *The Pet Beast* is one of content rather than of form, so the chief interest of the novel is primarily of content. Burgess's principal concern is to develop a portrait of an artist and to relate the artist's work to his psychological and spiritual development. Reared a Roman Catholic by a large, dirty, sow-like stepmother, Enderby had soon been ruined for both religion and society. He marries Vesta Bainbridge, thinking that she represents his muse, only to discover after she has squandered the money that had come from his stepmother, that she and the old woman are indeed one. In Italy, on an unconsummated honeymoon, Enderby understands that his has been a search for a true mother, the one denied him at birth, a mother slim, beautiful, and good. His grotesque stepmother, with her hanging breasts and her dirty teeth, had stood between him and a normal life. So he had created a substitute mother for himself in his adolescent bedroom out of the past—history and myth. The creation had become his Muse, and he had lived on friendly terms with her while earning a modest reputation as a lyrical poet.

Vesta Bainbridge is called into being by Enderby's subconscious. On the first morning of the New Year, as he sits in a pub facing the sea, talking to old men who have outworn their usefulness, Enderby thinks that he sees his stepmother. He knows that she is safely dead—he is living on her money—and he thinks, fretfully, that there is no need for him to feel haunted. He sees her wraith again several times, and he becomes more agitated with each "encounter." Soon he is asked by a friend, 'Arry, to write a few poems to Thelma, 'Arry's waitress-inamorata, in exchange for the loan of a suit that he needs to go to London to receive a prize given by Goodby, a publisher-poetaster, for the best volume of poetry of the year. There Enderby meets Vesta, who offers him a job writing simple poems-as-prose for *Fem.* After seriously considering her offer, he decides to reject it. He composes a torrid poem for 'Arry's Thelma and a polite refusal for Vesta, but he confuses the envelopes so that Vesta receives the poem and Thelma, the refusal.

Mistaking Vesta for the personification of his Muse, Enderby allows her to change him. Vesta dresses him, feeds him, puts contact lenses on his eyes, and spends his stepmother's money. She marries him in a registrar's office and transports him to Rome for a macabre honeymoon, revealing in Rome that she too had been reared a Roman Catholic. Enderby soon sees through the disguise that Vesta wears; she is not his Muse but his stepmother, although slimmer, elegant, and seemingly desirable. She speaks as the old woman had, saying "och" and "Harry-boy." She eats and drinks constantly; cleans her teeth with bits of cardboard; digs in her ears with hairclips, leaving on them the waxy residue to stale and harden. And, as the old woman had done before her, Vesta attempts to return Enderby to the church by marrying him properly in a church service. The most horrifying scene in the novel is that in which Vesta traps Enderby into attending a papal audience in Frascati. Enderby steps among, on, and over the devout and prayerful to escape the humiliation of kneeling before the figurehead of the church he has abandoned.

He finds a bar, drinks Frascati, and is soon joined by a railing Vesta. Caught in a summer storm, he is made further aware of the new identity his stepmother has assumed; for Vesta too, like Enderby's stepmother, is terrified of thunder, which is, after all, the voice of the god from *The Pet Beast*. When he decides to abandon Vesta in Rome and to return to England and his Muse, Enderby reasons that the money Vesta has spent has been returned to the old lady who had left it temporarily to him. He has enough, however, to mollify his Muse for a year or so, to return to a life of devotion to art. Back in England, settled in another resort on the sea, he discovers that his Muse has abandoned him.

It is Rawcliffe, a poet whose one decent poem has made its way into all the fashionable anthologies, who first causes Enderby to doubt himself. Warned by Vesta that Rawcliffe is jealous, Enderby nevertheless asks him to describe the departure of his poetic gift. In harrowing fashion, Rawcliffe details his ostracism from the Garden of Eden, the poet's ground: "one night there was the sound of an awful *click,* and then everything in the bedroom seemed cold, somehow, cold and obscene. I knew ... it was all over. Thenceforward I should be outside the Garden, useless to anyone, a mess, and, moreover ... in some indefinable way *evil.* Like an unfrocked priest.... The unfrocked priest does not become a mere neuter harmless human being; he becomes *evil.* He has to be used by something, for supernature abhors a supervacuum, so he becomes *evil*..." (200).

In London, Enderby had made the mistake of telling Rawcliffe the gist of *The Pet Beast.* In Rome, he makes the additional mistake of listening to Rawcliffe's drunken musings about the evanescence of the lyrical gift. He gives Enderby two tickets to attend the premiere of a film that he, Rawcliffe, has worked on, a film called *L'Animal Binario,* the two-natured beast. As he and Vesta watch the plot unfold, Enderby realizes that Rawcliffe has stolen the idea of *The Pet Beast.* He watches the vulgarization of his plot, its inevitable conclusion: Dedalo, the artificer, and Icaro, his son, invent an airplane, bomb the museum, and fly into the sky where they develop engine trouble; they crash into the sea, destroyed by their own creations. Meanwhile, the film's lovers embrace over the ashes of a civilization. In

England, Enderby later watches the film earn popular success under the title of *Son of the Beast from Outer Space.*

His Muse unwilling to speak to him, the images in his brain refusing to yield pattern and harmony, Enderby goes to a doctor, thinking that he may be seriously ill. Assured by the friendly doctor that he has many years to live, Enderby determines to kill himself. He buys a large bottle of aspirin, cooks for himself a "last supper, a thin but savoury viaticum," emphasizing his dual role as priest and victim; and prepares himself for death (233). As he approaches "some ineffable Presence," he is forced to struggle back, for his stepmother materializes to stand between him and the end: "She swung tits like sagging moons at him, drew from black teeth an endless snake of bacon-rind, pelted him with balls of ear-wax and snuffled green snot in his direction" (235-36). When Enderby screams for help, he finds himself returned to the world of the living.

Convinced while in the hospital by an absurd tale told him by a dwarflike man, who had put a metal nut around his penis and had had to have it removed by the fire brigade, Enderby decides "that it might be possible for him to want, with certain inevitable reservations, to go on living" (243). With a psychiatrist's "help," he develops a new identity and attributes his Enderby existence to a prolonged adolescence that had happily produced some beautiful although minor poetry. Enderby becomes first Enderby-Hogg and then Piggy Hogg, a bartender—the apparent end of Enderby.

The most compelling aspect of *Inside Mr. Enderby* is the manner in which Burgess characterizes the poet-man. The portrayal, psychologically as well as symbolically apt, suggests the stuff of poetic inspiration as well as the means of creating the art object. The poems, concerned more with form than with content, that Burgess offers as proof of Enderby's greatness convince the reader that the antihero poet is indeed all that is claimed for him. Somewhat facetiously, Burgess introduces, in a humorous Prologue, Posterity, disguised as a schoolteacher shepherding children through Enderby's bedroom—the first proof that Enderby is indeed a poet. The antiheroic aspects of the character, obviously, allow Burgess to rail against a world that seeks to destroy the individual by cutting everyone down to a manageable size—the theme that he developed in a striking allegory in *A Clockwork Orange.* The antiheroic character also allows him to develop hysterically funny, "black-comic" scenes that delight while portraying the horror of life in an absurd world. In one such scene, Enderby collars an irate and stupid neighbor with his toilet seat; and, in the funniest scene of the book, Enderby and Thelma's Communist-godfearing husband, Walpole, kneel before the gas fire as though it were a tabernacle and pray for Enderby's reconciliation with Comrade God. On cue, as Walpole rages against "boor Joyce" society, Vesta enters to claim Enderby for the world of *Fem.*

There are, however, several aspects of the development of the novel's theme that appear disconcerting—the dismantling of a poet and his reassembly into another person for a particular purpose; or the reorientation into a "useful" society of a "maladjusted" individual who happens, incidentally, to be a real poet. Ironically, comically, blasphemously at times, Burgess combines and purposefully confuses Christian and Classical myth, as he had done in *The Wanting Seed.* The reader does not doubt that the fusing of the two myths is right, and he appreciates Enderby's emotional and intellectual response to the circuslike whoop-de-do of Catholic Rome on religious holidays. What does concern the reader is the movement back and forth between religious doubt and conviction, Protestant feeling and religious mockery, good and evil, humanity and inhumanity. The imagery of the novel, mostly dealing with birds, does not fully accommodate the discrepancies. The novel's ending, more "black" than comic, which emphasizes Enderby's decision to join the Church of England (because its ways are easier than those of other churches) as a final consequence of his social reorientation does not satisfy. The "black" horror of Enderby's end, although it should satisfy the thematic content of the novel, somehow does not. A true protestant (accent on the first syllable) at the novel's beginning, Enderby becomes a Protestant in the communion of the Church of England at the novel's end.

Inside Mr. Enderby is, nevertheless, a compelling novel and one of Burgess's very best. It is written with the angry voice of an angel. The characters are all sharply conceived: Vesta, with her thin and craving body, sublimating sex in food; 'Arry, with his incomparable dialect sayings; Mrs. Meldrum, the unsympathetic landlady; Rawcliffe, with his drunken and confused opportunism; Walpole, with his "boor Joyce" snobbery. All have real vitality, and all exhibit Burgess's keen awareness of the humanity beneath the eccentric and the grotesque appearance. The novel itself becomes the maze that the reader has to work through to confront the monster whose eyes are twin worlds of love. But the chief accomplishment of the book is Enderby himself. The reader follows him with sympathy and compassion as he moves antiheroically, smell by smell, through the activities of the book. Exciting in his dedication to Beauty and Truth, he maintains, like Keats, that they are, perhaps, after all one. The insights into the poet's craft and sullen art suggest the demonic as well as the angelic aspects of the creative experience. If the poet eats honey-dew and drinks the milk of paradise, why isn't the thrice-woven circle enchanted enough to keep the world from him? The reader cannot help but say, "Oh God, that Enderby should become Piggy Hogg!"

The antiheroic aspects of the characterization, furthermore, allow Burgess to move into a devastating satire of many aspects of contemporary civilization, the façade covering the labyrinth. Journalistic adulterations, religious fanaticism, half-understood political reliances, commercialized vulgarities called "art"—all receive a fair measure of caustic commentary. The comic ideas which bounce from the page are enchanting in their originality and disgusting in their emphases, as they are meant to be. They force the reader to an appreciation of what is right, and, most important of all, they confront him with a comically defined tragedy—the destruction of an artistic sensibility.

III   Enderby Outside

Perhaps reluctant to leave Enderby psychologically oriented and useful to society under the disguise of a barman named Hogg—although it is Enderby's mother's name, as well as that of a minor but respectable poet—Burgess returned in 1968 to the adventures of his own minor but respectable poet. Entitled in England *Enderby Outside* and included in the American edition with *Inside Mr. Enderby* under the joint title *Enderby,* the sequel is at one and the same time the continuation of themes struck and played in the first part, but also a startlingly different book. *Inside Mr. Enderby* had concluded with Enderby's despair in failing to rediscover his Muse; *Enderby Outside* concludes with the materialization of the Muse in the disguise of a young, seductive girl. Enderby's adventures had begun by the cold English Atlantic, and they end by that same sea, in Tangier. The narrative of *Enderby Outside* moves from a glossy London hotel bar called Piggy's Sty, briefly into Spain, and then culminates in Tangier with Enderby again in command of his poetic faculty.

Dr. Wapenshaw's reclamation of Enderby-Hogg had involved the immolation of the poetic sensibility, a sacrifice that Enderby had reluctantly admitted only after he was certain that the Muse had abandoned him. The attempted suicide at the end of *Inside Mr. Enderby* had emphasized the poet's role as both priest and victim and, to a certain extent, had fulfilled the theme of *The Pet Beast*. The insinuative vocabulary and suggestive imagery had prepared the reader for the ritual act of expiation; for Enderby had indeed abandoned his search for Truth, had sold out to Vesta Bainbridge by setting poems-as-prose for *Fem* magazine.

As *Enderby Outside* begins, the reader is informed that the past is once more "fastening its suckers" on Enderby.[6] A hard-drinking worldly Irish priest immediately identifies Enderby: "You . . . have the face of a man who's been a long time away from the altar. A Catholic face I said to meself as soon as I clapped eyes on it, and very guilty and shifty too with your self-knowledge of being in the presence of a priest of your Church and you with the boldness to be speaking of blasphemy and many a long year between yourself and the blessed sacrament" (41). The theme of guilt is thus given a double significance, for Enderby has begun to understand his treachery; and, with this realization, his poetic faculty has begun to reemerge.

Where *Inside Mr. Enderby* had dealt chiefly with the inner processes of the creative experience, *Enderby Outside* concerns itself with the rediscovery of self in order that the creative imagination might survive in a hostile world. The differences in perspective that characterize the two parts of the novel, for indeed *Enderby* is one whole and entire piece, are suggested by the epigraphs. The first is from Laforgue:

> —Let's go then, last of poets,
> Kept constantly within you will make yourself ill!
> See, the weather is fine, everyone is without,
> Then go and buy yourself two cents worth of hellebore,
> That will give you a short walk;

the second, from Rubén Darío:

> Still wait.
> The bestial element nourishes itself
> On hatred for sacred poetry
> And this blot rushes recklessly from race to race.

The first comments on the isolation of the poet, indicating his need to search within the world for and in which he exists; the second, on the hostility and fear which the poet inspires. The epigraphs as well as the opening sequence of *Inside Mr. Enderby* and the closing sequence of *Enderby Outside,* the visit of the schoolmaster and the snotnosed children to the bedside of the sleeping poet, not only lend, mechanically, a frame to the two parts of the novel, but also remind the reader of the chief aim of the poet, immortality.

In addition to these obvious means of integrating the two parts that constitute *Enderby,* unity is achieved with contrasts that characterize Enderby inside and outside; the inner processes are examined in the first half; and the absurd outer world, the labyrinth that the poet must work his way through, in the second. Structurally, *Enderby* is, to date, Burgess's most finished achievement and his most original accomplishment. The comic patterns and rhythms of the novel, the imagery and moods, emphasize the theme; and the comic inventions fulfill the plan of the whole.

As in many previous novels, religion and society are mercilessly satirized, this time through Yod (suggesting the Hebrew character for Jehovah as well as the hands of man) Crewsy, a phenomenally popular "rock" singer managed by Vesta Wiggenstein, formerly Bainbridge-Enderby. A rude pun—the "pop" group is called The Crewsy Fixers—sets the comic tone. Piggy Hogg mixes out of barroom leftovers and slops a drink he christens the "Crucifier." When Yod Crewsy reads some of his poetry to an assembled group of bigwigs, politicians, and hangers-on, Enderby recognizes the poems as his, realizing that Vesta has appropriated his left-behind works. He wonders about plagiarism. Yod Crewsy is shot by a spurned member of the "rock" group, Jed (also suggesting Jehovah) Foote; and the gun is thrust into Enderby's hand. He escapes to Tangier by means of an economy charter flight. On the plane, and later in a hotel room in Spain, he finds himself involved with a selenographer, Miranda Boland, and he discovers, to his embarrassment and to her chagrin, that poetic inspiration comes at awkward moments. Enderby begins to dream of a new volume of poems, but Miss Boland refuses to understand that a poet's first mistress is his Muse. Throughout Enderby's journey of evasion from the police, in reality his journey of discovery, he follows the newspaper accounts of Yod Crewsy's decline and "death"; but it comes as no real surprise to the reader that the "pop" singer is "resurrected" toward the novel's end. The resurrection of the singer and the rebirth of the poet do, however, uncomfortably coincide.

In Tangier, Enderby meets Easy Walker, a soldier of fortune, devotee of the sonorous but hard-to-decipher poetry of one Ricker Sugden. Enderby learns from Walker, who reminds the reader in many ways of Nabby Adams, that Rawcliffe, the old Nemesis who had stolen *The Pet Beast* and translated it into *L'Animal Binario*, owns a seaside bar and café, El Acantilado Verde (The Raw Cliff). Enderby decides to destroy Rawcliffe, to whom he attributes his poetic difficulties. Once he sees the dying but unrepentant Rawcliffe, however, Enderby's resolve fades, replaced by a grudging compassion for and understanding of the dissolute man. Enderby discovers that Rawcliffe's degenerate life is the result of his being abandoned by the Muse: that Rawcliffe had indeed killed himself slowly through drink and debauchery, as he, Enderby, had attempted to kill himself with an overdose of aspirin. After Rawcliffe's death and his "sea burial," Enderby takes possession of Rawcliffe's bar-café and, to a certain extent, of Rawcliffe's identity. He renames the bar La Belle Mer, after the sea and after his stepmother; and he settles down to a life of disagreeable food and poetic composition.

Perhaps the most interesting and least successful of Burgess's "inventions" in *Enderby Outside* is the materialization of his poet's Muse: "The door opened and a girl came in, very tanned. She wore, as for high summer, a simple green frock well above her knees, her golden arms totally bare" (201). The girl immediately understands Enderby's difficulties, offers herself to him, an offer he Prufrockianly declines; encourages him to further activity; proves to be a severe judge of quality; eats like a truck driver; and disappears, but not before promising to return. And Enderby is left waiting within sight and sound of the Atlantic, knowing that "Whatever the future was going to be about, things ought to be all right, namely not too good, with enough scope for guilt, creation's true dynamo" (231).

CHAPTER 7

Back and Forth: East and West

I Honey for the Bears

WHEN *Honey for the Bears*[1] was first published in the United States in 1964, the year after its appearance in England, it met with mixed reviews. Several critics[2] took issue with Burgess's handling of the Russian scene and with his use of Russianized English and American "bop" talk; but what most distressed many was the fact that the book dealt with a homosexual theme in what appeared to be a pornographic manner. Christopher Ricks, in *The New Statesman,* admitted an admiration for Burgess's comic talent; but he also suggested that *Honey for the Bears* smacked of political and sexual subversiveness. He found Burgess supporting a "Third Force" in the novel, one that in some way combined satires of both Russian and American political principles, as well as of male and female. Ricks also suggested that Burgess was advocating homosexuality in the novel: "That homosexuality is not wicked, not ethereally spiritual, not necessarily the source of anxiety or agony, not incompatible with other things, but a rather pleasant virtuosity—if this be not subversive, what would be?"[3]

Although *Honey for the Bears* does consider Russian and United States politics and ideologies, and although sexual ambiguity is one of the concerns of the book, Burgess's novel neither condemns Russian or American politics nor endorses homosexuality. Rather, the conflicting ideologies and the ambiguous sexuality of the major characters become a flamboyant means of exposing a basically simple theme. As in his previous books, Burgess portrays the preponderance of evil over good; he stresses the duality of good and evil, and the fact that man is constantly buffeted between these two extremes. What makes Russians and Americans the same is their humanity: all men are implicated in the constant struggle of good and evil, yet evil seems to be constantly in the ascendancy.

The problem that *Honey for the Bears* poses is not one of political rights and wrongs, capitalism versus socialism, but one of human awareness. If "America's ... only a kind of Russia," separated by time rather than by space, it is because both countries are implicated in a primeval calamity (172). In a world threatened by an atomic holocaust, there are references made constantly to this ultimate evil—"Jackie Kennedy blowing the whistle and letting the Bomb drop"—in a world in which political opinions and convictions are ambivalent. And, in a world in which Orwellian "double-think" is common, it is no wonder that individuals are confused about their sexuality (153). Therefore, homosexuality becomes a metaphor for the contemporary world in Burgess's comic parable.

An antique dealer from West Sussex, Paul Hussey, together with his wife Belinda, is attempting to sell twenty dozen drilon—synthetic fiber—dresses on the Russian black market. Paul's ostensible reason for becoming involved in this illegal activity is to help his friend Robert's widow, Sandra; however, his real reason is soon disclosed—during the war, Paul and Robert had been, briefly, lovers. To fulfill some kind of emotional commitment, Paul and Belinda have come to Russia, and the novel's epigraph suggests this aspect of the journey: "We shall meet again in Petersburg, as though we had buried the sun." Paul and Robert had studied Russian and had also listened together to the music of Opiskin, a now-discredited Soviet composer. The past, as in all of Burgess's works, determines the present.

Hussey discovers soon from Dr. Sonya Lazurkina that what he had considered "innocent" wife-swapping—he and Sandra, Belinda and Robert—had in actuality been a four-square coterie; for Belinda and Sandra had also been lovers. The sexual ambivalence of the four friends is comically epitomized in the figure of Dr. Tiresias, whose head appears to be something that philosophy has unsexed, to be "some final Shavian achievement" (7). Actually a racketeer, Dr. Tiresias, whose original sex is always a matter of curiosity to Paul, believes that the day of the continuum is approaching, the day when there will be no more compartmentalization: "I think we must move on. . . . Towards the East. I am tired of categories, of divisions, of opposites. Good, evil; male, female; positive, negative. That they interpenetrate is no real palliative, no ointment for the cut. What I seek is the *continuum*, the merging. Europe is all Manichees;

Russia has become the most European of them all" (216). And
Paul is reminded of Bertrand Russell, sitting among students in
Trafalgar Square, when he looks at Dr. Tiresias; he is reminded
also of Yeats among school children; of Lady Gregory; and of
bisexual Lilith "from which Adam and Eve were, in paltry seg-
mentation, feigned apocryphally to derive" (212).

Paul soon discovers that Tiresias's business is to enable a few
to exchange so-called oppression for so-called liberty. But, if
Russia and America are one country, oppression and liberty
mean little. Zverkov, one of the Russian policemen who pursues
Paul as Paul attempts to get rid of the dresses, philosophizes to
him of the approaching time of union: "The winter has come
with its long nights" (255). When Paul answers that the winter is a long way off, Zverkov admits that this may be so for
little countries such as Finland, Sweden, Monte Carlo, and England, but not for the larger countries: "Dark dark dark. You
will have to seek the sun and you will find only with us or with
the other people across the Atlantic the heat and light you need
to go on living. The big countries, the modern states. Soon it
will just be one state" (255).

Early in the novel Paul feels a "pentecostal wind blow through
him" as he stands and asks a question about Opiskin of the
group that is assembled on the *Isaak Brodsky* listening to the
music of the Soviet composer Korovkin (10). As the ship approaches Leningrad, he looks at the land and is amazed to discover that Russia is colored like other countries, that it is not
all black and gray as it appears in spy films. While his wife
Belinda sleeps below because of a mysterious rash that has
begun to torment her, Paul finds himself involved in an anti-
clerical and macabre dance, a dance more surrealistic than
real; for, although it appears ludicrous, it is yet meaningful. On
behalf of all the first-class passengers, Paul protests against the
crudely offensive blasphemy; but he is put down. The young
people, a girl who looks like a fallen angel, a boy in a bishop's
miter, attempt to force Paul to a confession; and he admits that
it is right for him to be punished for the mysterious guilt which
he feels: "One of the two dialectical angels within him urged
that it was always as well to accept punishment when it was
offered.... It might help with this vague guilt about Robert,
whom these louts called Opiskin..." (33).

Forced to leave Belinda on board ship, Paul goes to the

hotel to make his contact, a rendezvous arranged by Robert before his death. He soon realizes that the authorities are aware of his black-market plans, but the suitcases containing the dresses have luckily been left on the dock, Paul having scooped up the wrong two while desperately looking for a taxi to take him to his meeting with the racketeeer Mizinchikov. When Paul returns to the ship, he discovers that Belinda has been taken to a Soviet hospital; and he follows, to find her in the care of the formidable Dr. Lazurkina. Leaving the hospital, Belinda remarks that Leningrad appears "kind of anonymous," not like London or New York. Paul appreciates immediately her meaning: "It was all nameless the way everybody in a family was nameless; names were for strangers. All the shops and stores and warehouses were in the family" (82). The anonymous or the ambiguous is Burgess's chief concern, and pansexualism is simply part of his general plan.

When they arrive at the Metropol Restaurant, both Paul and Belinda are impressed by the Czarist decor that speaks eloquently of old solid Russia; but they are equally impressed by the fact that they see "автомат"—out of order—on many of the machines.[4] Soon they find themselves befriended by Alexei Prutkov, a Russian, born in Brooklyn, who is unsure of his allegiances. They eat together, and an initial communion is established. Alexei soon betrays his ambiguous political perspective: "It's the State that's to blame.... It's the State that wants to kill off everybody inside it just to show it's more powerful than they are.... Russia or America...whats the difference? It's all the State. There's only one State. What we have to do is to get together in these little groups and start to *live*" (92-93). Alex proclaims, perhaps too much, that living life and having a good time are the important things. But "How to live?" is the unspoken question.

The anonymity of the state is then paralleled by Burgess's method in dealing with the anonymity of the sexes; for Belinda returns to the hospital and to the Lesbian embraces of Dr. Sonya Lazurkina: "There is no reason why she should not go with women.... There is nothing criminal in it. Women are very good at giving sexual pleasure to each other without danger of unwanted conception.... For sexual pleasure it is man with man or woman with woman" (115). Dr. Lazurkina points out that Belinda is homosexual because Paul is so himself; the real

crime, she insists, is unwillingness to face reality. Paul remonstrates that his "affair" with Robert was caused by the tensions
of the war, and he insists that the "rational" doctor is being
unfair. "Fair? It is nothing to do with fair and unfair," she
answers. "All you people in the Western countries are full of
guilt, and it is always guilt about the wrong thing" (116). When
Belinda finds some sort of comfort in leaving Paul for Sonya,
she considers her new attachment love: "I suppose Love has
nearly disappeared in England and the United States of America because there are so many easier substitutes for it" (203).

Paul himself becomes involved with Alexei Prutkov and
Alex's bohemian friends. In attempting to learn from them the
secret of living, Paul confirms his knowledge that America and
Russia are the same, that "America and Russia would make a
very nice marriage" (152). During a jazz party, Paul decides
to emulate Pierre's feat in Tolstoy's *War and Peace*: he drinks
a bottle of vodka not from a third-story window but from a
window high up in the warren where he lives with Alexei. He
drinks while being held upside down, by one foot. The next
morning, sick with crapula and feeling like a Christus, seeking
for a drop of vinegar to alleviate the taste in his mouth, he is
told by Alexei how he had revealed his homosexual proclivities
to the group: "You tried your dirty sexiness on Pavel, and you
tried it on me, but all you got out of that was a big punch in
the gut, dig. . . . And then, . . . you said you were going to have
Opiskin" (160). Paul, however, remembers that he has privately
entertained doubts about Alex's own sexuality.

That Russia and America are alike in kind but perhaps separated by time is one of the most interesting considerations that
the novel develops. Belinda, named by her father for the heroine of Alexander Pope's *Rape of the Lock*, remarks on the old-
fashioned or quaint aspects of the city of Leningrad. When she
writes to Paul about her decision to remain in Russia and with
Dr. Lazurkina, she says that she feels that she has returned
home, "not the home I had but the home I should have had"
(204). As Paul drives through the city, he places the impression that has been escaping him: "Slums, wall-eyed windows
of decaying warehouses. Bradcaster when he'd been a boy . . ."
(223). He and Belinda establish, therefore, some sort of spiritual kinship with their own past in the Russian city.

A running argument on the subject of good and evil, guilt and responsibility, between Paul and the policeman Zverkov helps develop the same argument. At the novel's end, Paul tells Zverkov, as they listen to Sibelius's *Fifth Symphony*, surely used for symbolical meaning, that he is returning to England, toothless, wifeless, and unsure of his sexuality. He continues that he is returning to an antique shop, "to conserve the good of the past, before your Americanism and America's Russianism make plastic of the world" (256). Paul insists that the world will yet hear about freedom, but he doubts his words as soon as he utters them. Russia may be the place of discovery, but meaning is safely stored away in an antique shop in England.

To return to England, Paul goes to Dr. Tiresias for a small loan. He has been beaten by Alex and by the Russian police; his denture has been lost; and his self-respect has been all but destroyed by his wife's decision to remain with Dr. Lazurkina. Tiresias reveals his occupation when he suggests that Paul earn five hundred pounds by escorting a political refugee as far as Finland. Paul, it turns out, has a joint passport for himself and Belinda. The sexless doctor tells Paul that the person wanting to escape from Russia is Opiskin's son, and that the boy's desire for asylum is necessitated by the fact that the authorities persecute him because of his father. Paul succumbs to the lure: a strapping young man is transformed into a gruesome transvestite, and Paul once again finds himself involved with a mad world.

Discovered by the same two policemen, Paul enlists the aid of a group of Englishmen to help him and young Opiskin escape into Finland. In Hitchcock fashion, Paul and the boy, dressed in women's clothes, are safely taken off the ship. Later Zverkov informs Paul that the young man was not Opiskin's son but a notorious criminal who had committed many of the really vicious crimes. Zverkov tells Paul that he is too innocent; that he thinks of himself too much as a Don Quixote and a Sancho Panza; that, consequently, he has let a murderer escape: "Why it is so hard to take you seriously as a man who likes the bad better than the good is because you are very innocent. You are as Tolstoy thought all men were or should be. I cannot remember what" (252).

Honey for the Bears, although an extremely well written and superbly plotted book, is not totally successful. The argument on Manichaeanism that runs through the novel underscores the religious import of the theme, and the religious element

emerges forcefully as it does in previous works. Ambiguity is
the keynote of the novel, and the novel maintains its own
peculiar ambiguity. Everything that is suggested by means of
statement or metaphor or image is countered by another statement or metaphor or image that clouds meaning. At the novel's
end, when Paul speaks of freedom to Zverkov, he doubts his
statement immediately. Certainly this confusion is in keeping
with the thematic intention of the novel as a whole, but it leaves
the reader bewildered as to the purpose for bringing up the point
in the first place. The romantic strength of Sibelius's *Fifth
Symphony* serves a symbolical function at the end; and it is
perhaps the melody singing over the horns that suggests, ever
so tentatively, the note of hope.

A very funny book, *Honey for the Bears,* also indicates a
departure from the extreme horror and grotesqueness of the
"black-comic" books, notably *A Clockwork Orange* and *The
Wanting Seed* which immediately precede it. After the strength
and power of these two books, surely Burgess's most successful
ones, *Honey for the Bears* seems a welcome change of attitude.
But *Honey for the Bears* is perhaps somewhat too esoteric in
developing and illustrating its theme. A good deal of the humor
in the novel is occasioned by Burgess's Russianized pronuncia-
tions and his use of names. Paul Hussey in the novel is called
"Pavel Gussey," for the Russians seem incapable of pronounc-
ing the "h." The word "gussey" perhaps suggests, nautically, a
jack-flag and, consequently, the Union Jack. The name Opiskin
is also used metaphorically, for the word suggests a "mistake
in writing"; the mistake, is, of course, not one in writing but
one of identity. The name Dobronravov, the captain who restores peace on the *Isaak Brodsky,* means "good tempered," "of
good character"; and the name Zverkov—the kinder of the two
policemen who first follow, then interrogate, Paul—suggests
"savage beast"; the name Korovkin, that of the other policeman,
suggests "cow." "Prutkov" means "rod-shaped"; and Lazurkina,
although not a Russian term, suggests not only the azure color
but also the word "lazar."[5] All in all, Burgess manages to have
a good deal of fun with his interpolations of Russian words as
well as with his Russianized English.

There is much wit in the plot construction, and there are
many rich and meaningful allusions, as in *The Wanting Seed.*
The scene in which Paul flings his drilon dresses to the Russian

women to keep from being arrested by the Russian police is one of the funniest that Burgess has devised: the honey of the West is flung to a greedy East. The scenes in which Paul escorts the disguised young man onto the ship, pretending that the padded hulk is Belinda, not only add to the general ambiguity of the sexual theme but are in themselves enormously funny. The scene in which Paul tells the two strapping Russians his fanciful story of two great countries being one country is superb comedy; all the while he tells his story Paul wonders why another prisoner, "a third man," wears pajamas.

But *Honey for the Bears* is a comic parable; and, although it succeeds as comedy, it fails as parable. For the purpose of parable is to reveal meaning, not to confuse it. Dangerous over-simplifications that bewilder and obscure do not make the best material for parable. Casting Paul Hussey as the protector of tradition and meaning is a good idea, and the idea is reinforced by references to his antique shop, its wares, and their quality; by his wife's name—Belinda, Pope's brainless but beautiful heroine; by references to *War and Peace* and other books of the past; and by language. Burgess's ear for idiom and dialect is as superb as ever, but somehow even the sacramental function of language is vitiated.

II Nothing Like the Sun

When Ted Arden visits Denham in Japan at the end of *The Right to an Answer*, he tells a strange story that had persisted in the Arden family through the centuries: Shakespeare had been a disappointment to the Ardens, whom he resembled physically; he had left Stratford to get away from his father; he had carried on with a Negro mistress; he had contracted the pox; and, most important of all to Ted, he had promised to leave the Ardens money. The sale of the *Hamlet* quarto discovered among Ted's family effects is for Ted the simple keeping of a promise, although centuries late. Published in 1964, *Nothing Like the Sun*[6] was subtitled *A Story of Shakespeare's Love Life;* and it makes use of historical information as it develops the story of Shakespeare's early years.

In an essay, "Genesis and Headache,"[7] Burgess tells his readers about the difficulties encountered in writing *Nothing Like the Sun*. In January, 1963, he began work on the novel which he

had been contemplating for a number of years, planning to
publish the book to help celebrate the fourth centenary of
Shakespeare's birth. The title Burgess took from one of the
sonnets, and the Dark Lady's name he found acrostically arranged in another, FTMAH. He describes how he experimented
with Elizabethan language, and how he settled for a version
somewhere between what might have been Elizabethan and
poetic fancy. The imagery of corruption and disease that informs
many of Shakespeare's later plays suggests that Shakespeare may
have indeed learned about disease from having had syphilis, and
the pox could have very well been contracted from the dark
heroine.

Burgess writes that he planned the novel "as a binary movement with a brief epilogue" (31). Part I was to deal with Shakespeare's early life; Part II, with the more mature Shakespeare;
and end with the shock of syphilis. Burgess saw himself as the
narrator, somewhat drunk from *samsu* wine, perhaps addressing
a class of special students. The Epilogue, he says, was "murder-
ously difficult" to write:

I gave it a first-person narrator, but I wanted his identity to be
not directly that of my hero—rather my hero trying to speak through
the mediumistic "control" of the storyteller or lecturer, who was
myself. . . . What I wanted to present was the steady worsening of
WS's disease—which he sees as a figure of the decay of the State
and ultimately as a symbol of the inborn rottenness of the human
condition—and its culmination in the dream-appearance of a goddess
(in the form of the dark lady, but really a fusion of the final stage
of the disease and the tragic muse herself). She allows him to smell
the very essence of evil. (43)

Into the novel Burgess also placed several tricks and deceptions;
he sets a sonnet as prose, blank verse as prose. Despite the "fanciful" re-creation of Shakespeare, Burgess admits that a good deal
of real scholarship went into the writing, "to relate documented
events to the conjectural development of WS's character" (39).

Indeed, the portrait of Shakespeare, called WS in the narrative, is a most convincing portrait of the historical figure, yet
surprisingly little is said about the "great" poet, "loved," "re-
vered," "admired," "idolized," by scholars, readers, dramagoers,
and men of "culture" everywhere. What Anthony Burgess gives
his reader in this amazingly effective portrayal is an idiosyn-
cratic insight into a man; and the man described is the kind who

could have written *Hamlet, Othello, Lear,* and also *The Tempest.* In the course of the portrayal, the "word-boy's" excitement gives way to the young man's physical sensations, which give way to the considered and passionate love of the man, all of which produce an artist of such compassion as to be almost godlike. Burgess leaves the subject of his biography in 1599, the year that the Globe is built; and the reader knows that before WS lie *Hamlet* (in 1601 or 1602), *Troilus and Cressida, Othello, Lear, Antony and Cleopatra,* plays of dark passion briefly, yet meaningfully, illuminated by shatteringly brilliant rays of golden light. Indeed, WS becomes one of Burgess's most optimistic portrayals, for the portrait testifies to the existence of greatness in a world basically corrupt and ignominious.

Burgess takes liberties with and stretches facts, as is the prerogative of the writer of historical novels, in order to illuminate the character of his subject. Anne Whately becomes an early and innocent love. The tricked-into marriage with Anne Hathaway and the confusion over the entering of the bans is realistically described. WS's first experience with homosexuality is comically handled in terms of the Quedgeley twins and the *Manaechmi;* WS confuses their identity and reaches for the wrong twin. He returns to Stratford with the beginnings of a comedy of errors in his head and a plan to go to London.

The glover's son in London discovers that writing plays is very much a craft as is making gloves; five feet for five fingers. The Burbages, Alleyn, Kemp, Heminges, Condell, and Pope all figure within the narrative. Essex, Southampton, and Florio enter the playwright's life; and soon WS is writing about Adonis and Lucrece and earning an unsavory reputation for himself in Stratford. Southampton eventually lends the thousand pounds that WS needs to buy his share of the Globe, but Southampton steals the Dark Lady away.

Susannah and the twins Hamnet and Judith are born and reared in Stratford; and the father's concern for their welfare, especially that of the son, determines him to put his London-earned money into Stratford real estate. The purchase of New Place becomes the bourgeois' triumph over his birthright, for his vinegar mother has always complained that she had married beneath herself. Hamnet, whose name WS has chosen from the Bible (Ham, nevertheless, reminds him of the old story of the unhappy Prince of Denmark), lisps to his father about his

uncle Diccon; and the reader begins to perceive a possible human beginning for Hamlet's drama. When the son dies, WS
reacts in horror and disbelief; the coat of arms that his father
John later applies for comes to mean little to WS with the boy
gone. Later, Burgess makes use of the apocryphal story about
Shakespeare's brother Richard and Anne: WS goes to Stratford
and New Place to visit his family as the tipsy narrator warns him
not to.

Historical events crowd the background of the novel. The
threat of the Spanish Armada; Essex's victory at Cádiz; the
queen's royal favor affecting the lives of men and nations; the
threat of Lopez, Tinoco, and Ferrara, occasioning one of the
most memorable descriptions of drawing and quartering in
recent literature; the plague; Robert Greene's disfavor; Christopher Marlowe's death; George Chapman's influence on Southampton; Florio and his *Montaigne*; and many, many other events
fill the novel with bursting life and undeniable vitality. But
there is always WS in the foreground, struggling to keep alive,
wondering about his plays, taking pride in his craftsmanship,
worrying about where he will get the money to buy a share of
the new Globe.

The two significant influences on WS's life are, of course, the
bright golden boy and dark golden woman. Southampton—W. H.,
Harry Wriothesley—and the Dark Lady—Fatimah, as she is
called by some—come into WS's life, and each moves into the
other's life, occasioning imagery of a particularly poetic nature.
The most exquisite single image of the novel, and the one which
sets and describes the pattern of the book, appears in a diary
entry for May 25 of either 1595 or 1596; for the year is not given
and has to be determined by the references made to *A Mid-
summer Night's Dream* and *Two Gentlemen of Verona*: "I dream
of our somehow gravely dancing a pavane or sarabande, all
three, in whose movement the recoiling of the beast and the
angel may, in myself be accomplished. I would in some manner,
wish to share her with him, him with her, but perhaps only a
poet may think in these high terms, not understandable of either
the soul (giver) or body (taker). And so I wait to be told that
I lose both a mistress and a friend" (151).

The two loves come to represent the division in the man
that must be reconciled before compassion and wisdom can
be fulfilled in the artist. The lady Fatimah, splendidly brown

and golden rich, becomes for WS the beast's heaven "which is the angel's hell" (151); the golden boy represents the most holy sort of love, platonic and good, once the body's hunger is appeased. Yet the devil within reminds WS that admiring the beauty of the boy's golden form presages an impure love. Truly, Burgess's Manichaean bias is fully operative in his portrayal of Shakespeare, and the reconciliation of the angel and the demon into the artist is what the novel chiefly considers.

It is no wonder that both the tipsy narrator and the sympathetic reader find themselves identifying with the subject of the biography by the narrative's end. Even such a line as "center of my sinful earth" assumes a new significance in the light of Burgess's analysis of WS's Manichaean world. The need to struggle, to move toward the light, is constantly dramatized: "But there are plays to be written, images of order and beauty to be coaxed out of wrack, filth, sin, chaos," writes WS as, sighing, he takes his pen to work, eliciting order out of chaos (154).

Both the dark lady and the golden boy become means of achieving, in the final analysis, the vision of golden beauty that the boy WS glimpsed when talking with the old drunken Jack Hoby, years before in Stratford, in the time of innocence. Perhaps what Burgess is implying is that innocence can be misplaced but never fully lost; and surely this theme is by no means startling or new in literature. The male child that Fatimah conceives becomes Burgess's symbolic means of suggesting the perpetuation of the golden dream.

That Shakespeare underwent some sort of psychological crisis before the writing of *Hamlet* has become a cliché of scholarly criticism. An increasing seriousness, a clouding over, apparent to many as early as *Julius Caesar*, foreshadow the presentation of evil which is the basis of the later plays. Scholars have been wont to attribute this "new" way of looking at the world to an increasing awareness of man's nature. Theodore Spencer writes in *Shakespeare and the Nature of Man*:

On one side was the picture of man as he should be—it was bright, orderly and optimistic. On the other was the picture of man as he is—it was full of darkness and chaos. . . . Previously Shakespeare had used the traditional beliefs *descriptively* as part of the background— the sun is compared to the king, the human body is compared to the state—and there is no question as to whether the beliefs are true.

But in *Hamlet* they are not in the background, they are an essential
part of the hero's consciousness, and his discovery that they are not
true, his awareness of what theory taught and what experience
proves, wrecks him.[8]

What Burgess attempts to do in *Nothing Like the Sun* is to regard
with a religious focus the man who becomes the spirit of his age.
He redefines a religious perspective. If WS smells evil, he nevertheless acknowledges the existence of goodness; for his work
elicits order out of the chaos of human involvement.

What is most remarkable about Burgess's book is that Shakespeare is not looked at primarily as a poet, dramatist, or artist,
although the references, oblique and shadowy, do keep the
reader aware of the manner in which he earns his living. Rival
poets like Ben Jonson, Robert Greene, and George Chapman
are introduced, not as rivals for greatness, but as competitors
in business. There is no glamorizing of the subject; WS is shown
as a gentle (essentially a fact) and as a simple man easily betrayed by his affection for those he loves. Sadness is perhaps the
keynote of the characterization; and Burgess very wisely does
not allow himself to soar rhapsodically in descriptions of the
happier poems and plays that WS produces, or to thrill over the
tricky working out of some plot aspect or quirk of characterization. The references to the plays and sonnets are made simply,
as one would describe a tailor's or a plumber's work. Burgess
never forgets the bourgeois beginnings of a Stratford man who
feels it a duty to himself and to his heirs to invest his money
in real estate.

Essentially WS appears an unheroic man—unheroic as the
world views heroism. It is left to Essex and to Southampton
to convey the world view of the hero: WS remains essentially
the bourgeois. The most exciting aspect of the portrayal is that,
once having looked at Burgess's WS, Shakespeare becomes WS.
For Burgess helps to fix the character, just as Shakespeare himself helps to determine views of Antony and Cleopatra. No one
who thinks of the serpent of the Nile thinks of her first as she
was historically; it is Shakespeare's aging beauty, wrinkled deep
in time, pinched black by Phoebus's kisses, that he imagines.

The same sort of symbolical rendering that Burgess indulged in
in *The Wanting Seed* is used in *Nothing Like the Sun;* for the
Dark Lady, Fatimah as WS prefers to call her, conceives a son;
and she thinks that both WS and Southampton have fathered

him. WS assures her that this is biologically impossible; he believes, however, that the child is his, and that the child will find the sun; for Fatimah has arranged that he will return to the lands of the sun. The pox that Fatimah transmits to WS from Southampton also indicates the symbolical unity that Burgess achieves in the novel. Three principals are involved in an intricate but beautiful pavane or saraband that encompasses truth, beauty, goodness, and light; for such is the soul of art. But art is also made out of the stuff of the earth: sin, corruption, and putridity. The child, symbolically, is offered to the sun, to light. There are, furthermore, references to water that add to the religious dimensions. When WS rides to Bath to experience the healing water, the narrator writes: "What properties those Bath waters had I cannot say, but I was purged in wraith's thinness" (216). Indeed, the movement of the novel suggests an exquisitely wrought ballet, the three principals moving through intricate designs of grace and rhythm, supported by an ensemble that itself weaves intricate patterns among those of the principals. When the design is broken, the novel ends. The reader is left to the musings of a drunken and sympathetic narrator whose enthusiasm for his subject has betrayed him into identifying with the subject itself, and the references to pennies and eyes suggest that death to which all life moves.

Nothing Like the Sun is written in a heightened prose, perhaps meant to capture something of the rhythms of Elizabethan speech. When WS speaks with Fatimah, his speech is poetic and provocative; but hers is matter of fact and charmingly accented. Florio, Southampton's secretary, serves not only as a referent for the man of letters but also speaks significantly and quietly to WS of his duty to his youthful friend to see that he marries to carry on his family line. Burgess never forgets the enchanting power of the word, and each character speaks uniquely in the novel. The final episode of the six-part Epilogue is entitled *Subject Matter*, and Burgess suggests in it that the narrator is as intoxicated by words as he is by wine: "Oaklings, footsticks, cinques, moxibustion, the Maccabees, the Lydian mode (soft, effeminate), the snow goose or white-brant, rose-windows . . . a Girle worth gold . . . the Queen that's dead (bee, meadow, chess, Bench, regnant), imposts of arches, pollards, sea-fox and sea-hog and sea-heath, the sigmoid curve, cardinals, touchability" (223). And the novel concludes with the words, "My Lord."

The imagery of golden light and teeming dark supports and sustains the novel. From the time that WS listens to the tales of the sea told by land-bound Jack Hoby until he moves to the sunlit Globe itself; from the time he listens to old Madge's prophecy, "Catch as catch can./ A black woman or a golden man" (22), until he recognizes that God is a "roaring clown full of bone-cracking japes" (216); from the time he writes his first verses about his love's "married" black brows, until he learns that gods and goddesses do not descend, that they are immanent in the self (213); and from the time that he suspects that his full knowledge of himself will come through and from love, until he stops to exorcise a "bowing smiling wraith," who is Sweet Master Shakespeare, as he enters the Globe, his golden world, the imagery of light and dark persist, reminding the reader of the burden of life and of the terrible beauty of pain. The Globe itself becomes, startlingly and prophetically, the world that WS will conquer; for the sun glints meaningfully over the theater as he enters it at the novel's end.

III   The Eve of St. Venus

Written first as an opera libretto in 1953, then expanded into a play, *The Eve of St. Venus*,[9] published in 1964, is Anthony Burgess's attempt to shape the aspects of a masque or entertainment into the form of a comic novel. The components of the masque—allegory, compliment, spectacle—develop and support the theme suggested by the epigraph, "Tomorrow will be love for the loveless, and for the lover love." The occasion ostensibly being celebrated is the marriage of Diana to Ambrose, to be held on the morning following the night of the events that constitute the delicate plot. Julia Webb, attempting literally and figuratively to seduce Diana from her commitment to Ambrose; Jack Crowther-Mason, in Parliament and Ambrose's best man; Sir Benjamin and Lady Drayton, Diana's parents; and Reverend Chauncell, the local vicar, complete the cast of main characters in this charming parable about the power of love.

An antic masque is suggested by the domestics in Sir Benjamin's house—Spatchcock, the maid, and the delightful nanny, whose five husbands still delight her in memory, although she has difficulty distinguishing among them. The aspect of the grotesque and the terrible, common to many masques, is sug-

gested by Julia Webb's attempt to spirit Diana away from her
duty to Hymen on the eve of the wedding. But a Sicilian Venus
is actually celebrated in the novel—a Venus who influences the
direction and purpose of the piece. There are Jovian rain and
thunder; divine portents and omens; mysteriously blooming
night-flowers; heavenly music; a brightly lit Venerian sky at the
spectacle's end—the various aspects of the masque all contained
within a fragile and charming irony that distinquishes the novel.
And the prose constantly breaks into poetry. There is, also,
Burgess's marvelous facility with words; and he takes great
amusement in putting Joycean expressions into the mouth of
Sir Benjamin—"Clutterfist. Slipshop demisemiwit. . . . Decere-
brated clodpoles"—that both delight and amuse the reader (7).

The story that Burgess tells is based on a tale told by Burton
in *The Anatomy of Melancholy* (in the Third Partition, Second
Section, first member, first subsection): "which he got from
Florilegus, ad annum 1058, 'an honest historian of our nation,
because he telleth it so confidently, as a thing in those days
talked of all over Europe.'"

Assembled on Sir Benjamin's lawn are the badly carved
statues of Venus and several male gods who all seem to resemble
the Vulcan. The ill-sculpted lot are a gift to the Draytons from
Bernard Drayton, Sir Benjamin's brother, whom Lady Drayton confesses never having seen. Periodically, Bernard arrives
to visit Lord and Lady Drayton, goes to his room, falls into his
bed with a case of whiskey, and remains there for his entire stay.
Bernard had purchased the statues from a stonemason in Catania,
who had been induced to carve them by a fast talker; the lot
had been designed as heroic garden furniture, but the stonemason had unfortunately bred into the work his own squint,
which explains some of the warped comic perspective of Burgess's piece. The talker who had commissioned the lot had disappeared, leaving the stonemason's daughter pregnant, and the
statues unpaid for. As they rest on Sir Benjamin's lawn, Venus,
alone of the group, "smirking like a whore," and modeled on the
pregnant girl, appreciates the extraordinary nature of the
events about to ensue.

While attempting to ascertain which is Diana's ring finger,
her fiancé Ambrose experiments with Venus's outstretched hand.
As soon as his ring circles her finger, the goddess's fingers close
inward; and Ambrose discovers that he is married to Venus

Anadyomene. Immediately, her strange, fishy smell pervades the house. That night, as Diana and Julia prepare to leave, Ambrose, asleep in the nearby inn, discovers a woman in his narrow bed; she is Venus, who tells him that he cannot marry two women since England is monogamous. He rushes to Sir Benjamin's house to tell Crowther-Mason, Sir Benjamin, and the vicar, who has come to check on the morrow's hymns, what has happened. The smell of the sea overwhelms the precincts, as Venus demands her rights of marriage.

The Reverend Chauncell, who believes in diabolical possession, takes Crowther-Mason with him to the vicarage to fetch the book that contains the Latin rites of exorcism. But, when the vicar attempts to read the formula of exorcism, both Crowther-Mason and he remark that the words mysteriously transform themselves into a Lucretian hymn of praise to Venus. It is Crowther-Mason who understands why the Christian rites of exorcism fail to function:

You must . . . open your eyes to a shocking heresy. Shocking because it's true. A new religion, as I see it, is not concerned with merely superseding the old but with enclosing it as well. Enclosing it. Containing it. . . . Truth, I should think, is not a matter of slow distillation but a cumulative revelation, weaving wider circles . . . rejecting nothing that's good, folding more and more beneath ever-widening wings. Good, however limited, can never be washed away by a greater good. Good can't cast out good. We talk about washing down bread and cheese with beer, but that isn't really so. The cheese becomes more alive, more significant, in that palatal consummation, sanctified as it were, with a glowing halo of hops and barley. . . . If you see what I mean. (95)

Crowther-Mason makes the point that the vicar has failed to free Ambrose of Venus's claim because the influence of the goddess is for good; for Love, whatever form it takes, is sacred. To discard the past because it is the past amounts to folly; for the present is made richer by the past, "and the past is made richer by the unfolding present" (95). The ancient gods are still alive, and their existence is not to be denied.

Summoned to new life by the marriage claim of Venus, the gods begin to exert their influence on the characters in the masque: Diana leaves with a Julia who is shocked to discover that Ambrose drunkenly boasts of having slept with a goddess; but a fierce thunderstorm and a tire punctured by a dartlike

arrow return Diana to her family. The same storm demolishes
the statues in the garden, and the spinster maid Spatchcock soon
returns the ring that began all the difficulty. The ring had been
brought to her window by a dove who carried it around its
neck by a loop of golden hair. But Spatchcock had thrown the
goddess's hair away. Ambrose at first, intoxicated by having
been the beloved of a goddess, refuses to go through with the
wedding; but he is soon convinced to do so. And the domestics—
the old nanny, still dreaming of life and love, her eye on the
male statues; Spatchcock, virginal and dour and hopeful—watch
as the principal characters meet in the night under the bright
star of Venus to celebrate the coming of Love. Even the respectable and dried-up Crowther-Mason experiences a reawakening
while an epithalamium is sung.

The main characters of the masque sing of Love as the marriage day approaches. Each singer weaves his own particular
refrain upon the love theme:

> Tomorrow will be love for the loveless, and for the lover love.
> The day of the primal marriage, the copulation
> Of the irreducible particles, the day when Venus
> Sprang fully-armed from the wedding blossoms of spray
> And the green dance of the surge, while the flying horses
> Neighed and whinnied about her, the monstrous conchs
> Blasted their intolerable joy. (124-25)

All the disquietudes of the evening are forgotten as the hymn
to Venus is sung on the evening of her canonization; for it is
indeed the celebration of an old, though new, saint that takes
place in Sir Benjamin's garden amidst the rubble of his brother's
broken statues. Admitting Love commits the characters to life;
and this admission is indeed a rousing one. The vicar, who
had abandoned his beliefs when he had proved ineffectual in
exorcising what he thought to be evil, returns to his ministry
with new zest as Diana and Ambrose contemplate their wedding day. Julia Webb returns to undertake her function as chief
bridesmaid; and Diana joyfully accepts her, knowing full well
that she could not live her life denying Julia's friendship.
Crowther-Mason, who serves as Chorus, or perhaps Master of
Ceremonies, is enchanted by the freshness and vitality of the
entertainment. Comically, as the family retires, Spatchcock, the
maid, turns to Diana and says, "If you'd do me a small favor,

Miss Diana, would you tell Sir Benjamin that them statues being broken was not my fault, Miss. Honest, I swear" (134).

An Epilogue of sorts concludes the graceful revel. Corruption and evil have been temporarily banished by the power of love; but the approaching new day brings the problems and concerns of the world beyond the garden where a Sicilian Venus had toyed with an English lover. Strangely, it is left to Sir Benjamin to speak the final words about the activities of the night. Characterized primarily by an obtuse cheerfulness, his chief concern is to get rid of the enormous quantities of food and drink purveyed for the wedding; and, as he looks out of his window into the garden, three bottles of burgundy perhaps help influence his thoughts: "The future was eating into the past, and he dreaded the future. . . . He was hearing all sorts of prophecies of doom these days, and he could well believe them. The world seemed bent on smashing all its mirrors. The world was building a hall of mirrors only to see the much-multiplied image of itself shivering into fragments, the narcissistic smile turned into a distorted leer" (135-36). The morning's newspapers, he knows, will tell of earthquakes and famines, "the unkillable widening grin of the pullulating East, the expanding machine of the almighty infallible state," anarchy, the anesthetic of mass entertainment (135). And yet the morning brings a wedding, a beginning.

The Eve of St. Venus is another change of pace for Burgess, but the same themes that inform and direct all of his works are apparent in the parable. The power of love, presaging goodness, here almost thwarted by the evil of the world, is delicately and comically portrayed in the guise of a graceful entertainment. Julia Webb, her name implying her function in the spectacle, almost attains her ends: the fly in her web of death. But love proves more powerful than her skein of evil; and the golden ring of Venus's hair, the circle encompassing the web, suggests, as in *The Worm and the Ring*, the power of the marriage contract over the forces of dissolution.

Yet the same old Manichaean world exists outside Sir Benjamin's garden, and in the final pages of the novel the funny old man recognizes the fear that resides outside the cheerful circle of his own marriage. Julia Webb, a developed version of the antiheroic personality, is characterized by her "naked hungry

will" (45). But she too is overwhelmed; and she submits, temporarily, as the final scene implies, to the promising marriage of
Diana and Ambrose. Although the triangle relationship, so consistently used in the majority of the novels, figures prominently
in *The Eve of St. Venus,* the circles of the wedding ring and
of Venus's hair best symbolize the unity that Burgess is attempting to portray. The reader is thankful for the circle, however,
because it gracefully, forcefully, and poetically suggests that
there are moments of revelation that do give life balance. Of
course, an epiphany is portrayed in many of the more serious
novels; but horror and fear, compressed into tight "black-comic"
metaphors and fearful surrealistic scenes sometimes subvert the
optimism; and the devil of the world seems frequently too powerful to oppose.

IV   Tremor of Intent

In the third Canto of the *Inferno,* Dante considers the sin of
Sloth, or Acedia. He likens those who could make no decision
for good or evil to the Laodiceans; neither hot nor cold, they
are the most despicable of creatures. Consequently, both heaven
and hell reject them. The slothful are tormented immediately
inside the gates of hell: their punishment is to rush eternally
back and forth after a banner that forever eludes them. Beyond
this vestibule where they are punished, flows the Acheron, its
bank crowded with the numerous lost souls who await their
transportation to the various punishments assigned them by a
just God. Dante, alive, cannot be transported across the river
of the dead: he faints, then awakens to find himself mysteriously
on the other side. The sinner who is trying to better himself
mysteriously receives the help of God.

In Anthony Burgess's, *Tremor of Intent* (1966),[10] the slothful
are referred to as the "neutrals"; and their place in contemporary
cold-war politics is comically assessed. The cold-war and the
espionage activities of the novel become mere copies of the
war between what Burgess refers to as God and Notgod: "Salvation and damnation of equal dignity, the two sides of the coin
of ultimate reality" (237). Those engaged in the cold war between East and West, for good or evil, are better than the neutrals; for they are aware of the two extremes: God and His
opposite, or what Burgess consistently refers to as the "great

opposition." Manichaean duality in *Tremor of Intent* affords
the pattern for what Burgess calls an "eschatological spy novel";
and his concern is with ultimate realities: God, the Devil, Hell,
and Heaven. In other words, he is concerned with theological
considerations, free will and salvation.

Tremor of Intent uses the devices of the contemporary cold-
war spy novel in order to develop and illustrate its themes. Consequently, it calls to mind the thrillers of Ian Fleming, John Le
Carré, and Len Deighton. Burgess's protagonist, Denis Hillier,
stands midway between Le Carré's Leamas and Fleming's 007;
the bourgeois beginnings suggest both Harry Palmer and Leamas; and the interest in athletic sexual play and gastronomic
expertise suggests James Bond. A Graham Greene influence is
also to be detected in the characterization of Denis Hillier,
apart from the Roman Catholic background: in *The Third Man*,
Rollo Martins searches for old school-friend Harry Lime, whom
he discovers in an "unreal city," bombed-out Vienna; in *Tremor
of Intent*, Denis Hillier makes a quixotic search for Edwin Roper.
And there is, as always, the influence of James Joyce which
cannot be overlooked: the interest in language and in ritual
reminds the reader constantly of both *Ulysses* and *Finnegans
Wake;* indeed, Father Byrne, the anti-Semitic Irish priest, with
his mind on sex, surely suggests the Irish priests of *A Portrait
of the Artist*—as well as Evelyn Waugh's Father Rothschild in
Vile Bodies.

But again, as in all of Burgess's previous novels, influences and
similarities mean little when compared with the startling aspects
of the fable and with the marvelous ingenuity of the comic devices. Denis Hillier emerges in *Terror of Intent* as Burgess's
strongest protagonist, for he is convincing in two roles—as a spy
engaged in cold-war activity and as a soul wandering among the
uncertainties and bewilderments of a world that is essentially and,
perhaps, irredeemably doomed. For, at the end of the novel,
after Hillier has spoken to Clara and Alan Walters about the
necessity of identification with either the camp of God or that of
Notgod, its opposite, he appears unsure. He thinks of acedia,
feels hungry, and goes with his friends to have a good dinner.
Yet, because Hillier's final word is "Amen," the reader is left
to interpret as he will (240).

In *A Vision of Battlements*, Ennis goes with Agate to hear the prophecy of Mrs. Carraway, the sybil. Mrs. Carraway looks reluctantly into the future and unwillingly reveals her vision of a man dressed in clerical garb. She refuses to tell Ennis whether the man is himself or not, insisting that the face is not clear to her. In *Tremor of Intent,* it comes as no real surprise to the reader that Hillier has become a priest by the novel's end. The time factor—study, ordination, and so on—is neatly glossed over: a little over a year after the main activity of the novel Hillier meets Clara and Alan Walters and reveals his new identity. The reader is reminded of the way that Dante mysteriously found himself on the other side of the Acheron after recovering from his faint.

In *Honey for the Bears,* the expression "tremor of intent" is also used. Paul Hussey takes a drink of Old Mortality, the same whiskey that Hillier is served by the steward Wriste in *Tremor of Intent.* Paul thinks of his wife, his loss, and his uncertain sexual identity; and he sees himself as the keeper of an empty antique shop. The "tremor of intent" within the context of *Honey for the Bears* suggests, very tentatively, a spiritual yearning, as it does in this book. The expression is perhaps taken from García Lorca's *Bodas de sangre,* from the speech of the mother:

> Neighbors; with a knife;
> with a tiny knife,
> on a divided day, between the hours
> of two and three,
> the two men were killed for love,
> with a knife
> with a tiny knife
> that hardly fits the hand
> but which penetrates finely
> through astonished flesh,
> and stops in the place
> where the dark root of a shriek
> trembles in organic nets.[11]

The tremor which Hillier feels as he for the second time approaches the voluptuous Miss Devi suggests the quaver of the spirit as well as that of the flesh.

For *Tremor of Intent* works on two levels: at one and the same time it is a suspenseful spy story and an allegory on the theme of responsibility and commitment. The two levels merge consistently and provocatively to make a novel that is both enter-

taining and theologically apt, always, however, within the general
context of a Manichaean universe. Free will, the choice for
God or Notgod, enhances the spy story but at the same time
insists on man's commitment to a code or belief that transcends
interests of party or nationality. Midway in the melodramatic
activities of the novel, Hillier asks Alan Walters if he has ever
thought of the nature of ultimate reality, if he has ever considered what lies beyond God. "Nothing's beyond God," answers
Alan; to which Hillier replies:

Beyond God . . . lies the concept of God. In the concept of God lies
the concept of anti-God. Ultimate reality is a dualism or a game
for two players. We—people like me and my counterparts on the
other side—we reflect that game. It's a pale reflection. There used
to be a much brighter one, in the days when the two sides represented
what are known as good and evil. That was a tougher and more
interesting game, because one's opponent wasn't on the other side
of a conventional net or line. He wasn't marked off by a special
jersey or color or race or language or allegiance to a particular
historico-geographical abstraction. But we don't believe in good and
evil any more. That's why we play this silly and hopeless little
game. (119)

The "silly and hopeless little game" is, of course, cold-war espionage, salvation and damnation.

Denis Hillier is sent by his superiors to rescue, or to forcibly
return to England, his old schoolmate and friend, Edwin Roper,
now a rocket-fuel expert working for the Soviet Union. Hillier
and Roper have in common their Roman Catholic education
which has badly prepared them to cope with a modern world
by deeply implanting in them a sense of guilt. Disguised as
Sebastian Jagger, a typewriter merchant, Hillier boards the
Polyolbion, a ship bound on a gastronomic cruise for Yarylyuk
on the Black Sea.

Hillier knows that he suffers from two serious moral flaws,
satyriasis and gluttony; yet one has managed to cancel out the
other, and he has retained the appearance of a debonair, cul-
tured man of the world. On board the ship he meets, almost
immediately, Clara and Alan Walters, who are accompanying
their tormented father and greedy stepmother on the cruise to
the Black Sea. The children are described as particularly obnox-
ious, especially the know-all boy, Alan, who has been on "quiz"
programs. Soon Hillier meets the large, bald, menacing fellow

passenger Theodorescu, who is accompanied by his secretary-
companion, Miss Devi, a voluptuous Indian. Wriste, a gumless
and ingratiating steward, completes the cast of main characters
involved in the espionage aspect of the novel.

The first part of the novel is a "letter" addressed to Hillier's
superior, a letter which he neither writes nor sends. The purpose
of the letter is to acquaint the reader with the background of
Hillier's life, his relationship to Roper, his interference on Roper's
behalf with Brigitte, Roper's German wife whom Roper had
married out of a sense of guilt. Having seen the immediate after-
math of concentration-camp extermination, Roper, like the
Stone twins in *The Doctor Is Sick,* had felt a strange responsibility because the English had not suffered in such camps.
Brigitte becomes his means of rectifying an injustice done to the
tormentors by those tormented—a strange kind of logic indeed,
but one that is understandable within a Roman Catholic appreciation of the nature of guilt and responsibility. Brigitte, it develops, is a prostitute; and Hillier, asked by Roper to avenge
his friend's cuckoldry, becomes himself involved with Brigitte,
who has previously referred to him as a "fiend." When Roper
joins the Labour party after Brigitte leaves him, he finds her
again practicing her trade among important politicians; and he
blackmails Cornpit-Ferrers, one of her clients, into forcing her
to return to him. Roper's defection to the East, arranged by
Cornpit-Ferrers, is more an expediency than a matter of intellectual conviction.

When Hillier is asked by his superiors to return Roper to
England by any means he can, he has already become disen-
chanted with the spy game; the betrayal of a fellow spy named
Martinuzzi by their employers has convinced him to retire from
active espionage. What Hillier does not realize, despite several
signs, is that his employers also wish to get rid of him; for he
knows much too much about the English espionage system to
be allowed to retire from the service. (Here Burgess, of course,
models his plot on that of *The Spy Who Came in from the Cold.*)
In a dream that Hillier experiences, after concluding his imagi-
nary letter to his employer, the ending of the novel is fore-
shadowed: "The coolness exorcised that small bad dream he'd
had—the buffeting with rose branches, the yelling crowd, his
breathless crawling up a road that grew steadily hillier. That,

of course, was a dream of his own name; a huge coil of rope he'd been carrying was explained by the name of his quarry" (53). What Hillier fails to appreciate is the scapegoat or Christ imagery that underscores the dream. The reader of the spy story, however, begins to suspect the ending, and the scapegoat motif triggers the allegory.

Roper, it develops, does not want to return to England. Wriste, Hillier's cockney steward, turns out to be a paid killer in the employ of Panleth, a world-wide extermination agency, who has been commissioned to kill both Roper and Hillier. Theodorescu, however, has secured information from Hillier by having Miss Devi inject him with a truth serum while having intercourse with him. Alan Walters rescues Hillier, after he has given up hope of rescue and has become reconciled to death at the hands of Wriste, who engages him too long in eschatological debate before inflicting the coup de grâce. Young Alan had managed to secure a gun by submitting himself to Theodorescu's homosexual appetites, and he uses it to destroy Wriste, whom he had spotted as an impostor much earlier on the Polyolbion. Alan shoots Wriste through the eye (the one-eyed sailor), and then becomes promptly ill; his shoulders heave as he throws up the modern world. Hillier carves his own tell-tale "S" mark into Wriste's leg, and he mutilates the killer's face in an attempt to confuse his opponents into thinking that Wriste has completed his mission for Panleth.

When Hillier goes to Istanbul to find Theodorescu, he is intent on killing him for his part in the betrayal. He finds Theodorescu, gratuitously gives him much secret information, and then attempts to shoot him. But Miss Devi has taken the precaution of removing the bullets from Hillier's gun. Hillier grabs his hypodermic, follows Theodorescu down the stairs as the fat gangster descends in the elevator, injects him with a drug and then leads him to the sea and to death by water. A few months later, while sitting in a pub in which a television documentary on a great Irishman (Joyce?) is being made, Hillier reads in the Times that Alan and Clara would like to see him again. He writes that, in a year's time, he will communicate with them. When they arrive, he reveals that he has become a priest. Thus the prophecy made by Mrs. Carraway to Ennis, whose brother under the skin Hillier is, is fulfilled.

The plot of the novel is exciting and suspenseful; the devices are sensational; the puzzle intriguing. The innocent children, Alan and Clara Walters, who are more concerned about their dying father and voracious stepmother than about cold-war espionage, add a note of earthy and fumbling gaiety to the novel. But, because of Hillier, they become implicated in the filth of existence. Furthermore, the novel is extremely funny, as Burgess indulges himself in the name game that helps to reveal the subterranean meaning of his allegory: guilt, responsibility, compassion; God, the Devil, heaven and hell.

Theodorescu, whose Greek-Romanian name suggests a gift of god, is the chief "neutral"—a gangster who sells bona fide information to the highest bidder. A travesty of the omniscient and omnipotent God, he is a projection of the gangster-God that Burgess had described in *A Vision of Battlements*. He has prodigious appetites for food, money, and information. He knows everything about everyone; omniscience is his business. Miss Devi tells Hillier that Theodorescu is the discreetest man she knows, that he has gone beyond the need for women. Theodorescu himself tells Hillier that he prefers Greek shepherd boys, Ganymedes. Hillier indeed thinks of him as a god: he feels that Theodorescu has to look through only one eye in order to see, appreciate, and understand the basic urges of humanity. When Theodorescu challenges Hillier to an eating contest, he instinctively suspects Hillier's gluttony. In course after course Hillier and Theodorescu comically gorge themselves, each refusing to surrender to the other. Theodorescu wins the contest. Again, as in earlier novels, something of a black mass is suggested.

Soon Hillier finds his other dominant passion aroused. He goes to Miss Devi's stateroom—he had seen her earlier in her bath, and had felt like Actaeon looking at Artemis. With Miss Devi, he indulges in an orgy as consuming as the one he had had with Theodorescu. Miss Devi goes beyond the *Kama Sutra* in her knowledge of sexual bliss; Burgess comically suggests that her manual is the rare Pokam. At the end of the orgy, Theodorescu enters, informs Hillier that he has been drugged, and showers money over Hillier's nakedness—the shower of gold is surely another manifestation of the god. Wriste returns Hillier to his stateroom and to his bottle of Old Mortality.

The authorities are warned of Hillier's presence on the ship

by Miss Devi; he is forced to enlist the help of Alan and Clara
to fulfill his mission. He does not yet know that he is the scapegoat. Clara uses her charms to snare a Russian officer: Hillier
overpowers him, injects him with a drug, takes his uniform,
and leaves to find Roper. Theodorescu and Miss Devi, however,
have left the ship by helicopter—still another manifestation of
the god. The god ascends in his machine. Later on, when Hillier
finds Theodorescu in Istanbul, he catches him as the elevator
descends to the ground floor of the hotel; the god descends for
the last time in his machine. Hillier hounds him to the Black
Sea, where Theodorescu dies quietly, talking of England and
his schoolboy days. Ironically, schoolboy days have brought
Hillier to the point where he must come to terms with himself.

Within the allegory, many of the names assume important
meanings. Theodorescu points out to Denis that his name is a
diminutive of Dionysus, which suits the grosser aspects of the
characterization. Hillier's pseudonym is "Sebastian Jagger": the
Sebastian suggests the Christian saint martyred by flights of
arrows; Jagger, the Dickens solicitor, Jaggers. Clara, whose name
means simply "light," is blonde and innocent; her innocence is
comically guarded by a cordon of weighty books on sex; and
she becomes to Hillier the angel of light, his Beatrice, his means
of securing paradise. He falls in love with her, as a boy would
with the Virgin Mary. Hillier kisses the hem of her garments
as he hides in her closet while waiting for her to bring the Russian
to him so that he can leave the ship. But the Dionysian aspect
of his nature makes him desire her physically. He sees himself,
furthermore, as her father, and incest becomes an exciting
temptation to him.

Miss Devi, dark, voluptuous, mechanical, and knowledge-
able—it is amazing how she can keep her mind on her work while
going through her many exotic postures of sex—suggests the mate
of Siva, god of destruction and reproduction. Her relationship to
Theodorescu is kept mysterious; but she comes, on a human
level, to resent the influence of Clara on Hillier when he refuses
her in Istanbul. The *Polyolbion* (a reference to Michael Drayton) suggests "many old things," but it is referred to once as
Perfidious Polyolbion. The pun is of course on Albion. And
finally there is the flexible Wriste, a far cry from the Len whom
Denham met in Colombo in *The Right to an Answer*. Wriste

is the hired assassin destroyed by his very pride in his work, his
pride in letting his victim fully appreciate the gratuitous theological aspects of execution. "Strange," says Wriste to Roper
and Hillier as he prepares to kill them; to prove that he has done
so, he will take one finger back to his employers:

... in a minute or so you will both be vouchsafed the final answer.
Religion may be proved all nonsense or completely vindicated. And
the Archbishop of Canterbury and the Pope of Rome cannot in the
least profit from your discovery. Top secret. Locked drawers. A safe
with an unbreakable combination. There may be a quattrocento
heaven, there may be a Gothic hell. Why not? Our aseptic rational
world does not have to be a mirror of ultimate reality.... The knowledge you are going to possess is the only knowledge worth having.
(169)

And he asks if Roper and Hillier want to pray. Hillier does, but
Roper does not. The rain that first stormed falls more gently
outside the gardenhouse where red rose bushes grow near by.
As Alan kills Wriste, he screams, "You bloody neutral.... You're
going where all neutrals go" (171).

The neutrals within the novel, then, are those who prey on
others; they are those who, having no commitment and gratifying
their egos, feed like parasites on the world of God and Notgod.
They are Theodorescu, Wriste, and the children's mother Mrs.
Walters, who succeeds in destroying her husband by forcing
him to overexert his weak heart in every way; and they include
Brigitte Roper and her politically important lover, Cornpit-
Ferrers. But Miss Devi, the opposite of Clara, escapes every
category. Hillier explains to Clara and Alan: "She had great
gifts. She was a door into the other world.... It wasn't the
world of God and Notgod. It was a model of ultimate reality,
shorn of the big duality however. In one way she purveyed
good, that other neutral. But good is a neutral inanimate—music,
the taste of an apple, sex" (238).

In *A Clockwork Orange*, Burgess illustrates the point that a
choice for evil was better than no choice at all. Programmed by
the Ludovico process to do nothing but good, fifteen-year-old
Alex became "a clockwork orange." In *Tremor of Intent*, the
argument concerning the nature of will is further elaborated,
but in more realistic terms. Hillier says to Theodorescu, before
they engage in the gorging contest, "I believe in man's capacity

to choose, I accept free will, the basic Christian tenet" (71). Theodorescu, who counters with a comic "Excellent," asks Hillier to choose the first course. Later, as Hillier is being coerced by Theodorescu to reveal the location of Department 9A of Intercep, Hillier realizes that Theodorescu wants him to reveal the information of his own volition. As he does so, Hillier begs forgiveness (99). After he kills Wriste, Alan accuses Hillier of being one of the neutrals; but Hillier knows he is not. He has thought, however, of becoming a neutral after his last dirty job for the department has been finished. At the novel's end, the reader finds Hillier within the Catholic Church; and one must assume that God has sent him grace to prepare for the Revelation which, in Hillier's case, means the acceptance of the discipline of the church that he had rejected intellectually but not emotionally. The reader remembers the letter that Hillier had composed to his superior, who is addressed as "Sir"; that the letter had been a going-over of the past in order to assess the present and the claims of the future. The shadowy "Sir" had suggested another sir. It does not, therefore, come as a complete surprise to learn that Hillier has chosen the life that he reveals to Clara and Alan in Ireland.

Running throughout the novel, one finds also the discussion of the nature of the evil that resides in the uncommited. "Evil," says Hillier to Theodorescu, "resides in the neutrals, in the unconvenanted powers" (219). Hillier's execution of Theodorescu therefore becomes, within the religious context of the novel, the destruction of evil, or an evil. Theodorescu drowns, but Hillier leads him to his death. One is reminded at this juncture of the novel's melodrama of the manner in which Graham Greene's Wormold manages to get rid of the spy Carter in *Our Man in Havana*: in both novels, the aspects of personal guilt and responsibility are wisely left undeveloped.

But the children Alan and Clara are ultimately of chief significance to the meaning of the book. Alan is introduced to evil by his neutral stepmother, and he is initiated into it by the homosexual embrace of Theodorescu. Alan's killing of Wriste, an act of intelligent volition, amounts to an attempt to rid the world of evil. Theologically, one concludes that Alan is pure; for he kills Wriste to save the lives of Hillier and Roper. Yet, like the pattern of the life of a Greeneien innocent, that of Alan's life is set. He becomes interested in medieval history in a period when, perhaps, the struggle of good and evil was less difficult to understand. Clara too is introduced to evil by her neutral stepmother, but she is initiated into it by her father-lover Hillier. Yet the two children who have never eaten bread until Hillier introduces them to it by the novel's end have learned to eat it. The cake/bread pattern suggests the Eucharist, the communion that the Eucharist symbolizes. Indeed, the bread breaking in all Burgess's novels implies, to a certain extent, the same intention.

Tremor of Intent, within the pattern of Burgess's artistic development, is one of his most successful efforts. The intrigue lends itself well as a framework for the theological problems considered. There are moments when the fable lurches into allegory; but, on the whole, the two patterns are well handled. There is the same irreverence in the novel toward sacred matters that one observes in the novels that precede it; but, with the character of Hillier, Burgess moves away from the flat, two-dimensional characterizations that he relied upon in his most successful "black-comic" efforts; namely, *Devil of a State* and *A Clockwork Orange.* The device of imposture is brilliantly used to develop Hillier's return to his church. The various names and ruses that he has used in his espionage have disguised him from himself; he rediscovers his identity when he feels that nothing or no one can save him from Wriste.

The destruction of Theodorescu is a freely chosen act on his part, an attempt to reorient himself into the world of ultimate meaning.

CHAPTER 8

Conclusions

ANTHONY Burgess's comic skill relies principally on the combination of the horrible and the absurd to achieve a proper effect. In the majority of the novels, horror and absurdity are balanced to achieve a comically appropriate moment. When the balance is tipped in favor of one at the expense of the other, the novel suffers. Comedy is, to say the least, the most difficult and most treacherous form in which a novelist can work, and the fact that Burgess has created a number of superbly funny books, ones in which horror balances absurdity in order for an underlying religious purpose to emerge cogently, is ample testimony of the fact that he is a master of this most difficult and elusive form.

Burgess admits to the influence of Evelyn Waugh on his work; but, in considering the overall effects and ultimate purpose, Waugh's influence seems less important to Burgess's method than at first appears. Exaggeration and absurdity serve Waugh well, especially in the early novels, from *Decline and Fall* to *Put Out More Flags*. Burgess's use of absurdity, although Waugh does indeed stand behind some of the hilarious scenes, relies more on Kafka's purpose and on Joyce's method than it does on Waugh's, principally because language is used to force the reader to an awareness of religious and/or metaphysical considerations. In his study of Joyce, *Re Joyce*, Burgess writes: "Most novel-readers want to get at the content of a novel without the intermediacy of a kind of writing that seems to obtrude, rivaling the plot in its claim to be looked at."[1]

Relying heavily on both Kafka's and Joyce's methods, Burgess approaches the novel with the same concentration that a poet approaches his craft. Language, denotative as well as connotative, is forced to yield new and startling dimensions of meaning, as it does in the poetry of Gerard Manley Hopkins and Rudyard Kipling. Occasionally the reliance on language escapes the pur-

164

pose of communicative prose and calls more attention to itself than to the feelings and implications that it should convey. Indeed, Burgess admits to being in love with language; and he indulges in all of his novels in his taste for the exotic and the surprising word. "Callipygous," "scataphagous," "borborygm," "lingamyoni," "dendropod," "acroamatic" are just a few examples of the words put before the reader both for his amusement and his consternation. In *The Doctor Is Sick*, the linguist's fascination with language becomes an integral aspect of the theme; and, in *Nothing Like the Sun*, Shakespeare, a "word-boy," is shown weaving the web of language to produce designs of wonder. In *A Clockwork Orange*, Burgess "invents" a language of his own—Nadsat—thus giving full play to his fascination or, perhaps, obsession. Other influences, besides those of Waugh, Kafka, and Joyce are apparent in Burgess's writing. Laurence Sterne, Charles Dickens, Graham Greene, Vladimir Nabokov, and numerous others could be mentioned; but the ultimate consideration is that Burgess refines all influences to suit himself, and the novels are marvelously his own.

In the majority of the novels, Burgess deals with the contemporary maladjusted hero. His concern with the antiheroic personality forces him to consider various complexities—satanism, romanticism, Machiavellianism; but his heroes ultimately gain in stature because they are pitted against the universe that is temporarily ruled by a gangster-God and predicated on what Burgess admits to be a Manichaean basis. Here the reader again encounters the influence of James Joyce, for Burgess writes that "The comedy of Joyce is an aspect of the heroic: it shows man in relation to the whole cosmos, and the whole cosmos appears in his work symbolized in the whole of language" (25). And he then defines the appeal of the mock-heroic protagonist:

Man is interesting and important enough to be examined in great detail and at great length, but he is not by any means Lord of the Universe. The universe can be a mystery or an antagonist: against it the comic-epic hero opposes all he has, and it is not much—merely free will and a capacity for love. His defeats are inevitable but always contain the seed of a victory that the universe, a vast mass of organized iron-mongery, is not equipped to understand. It is the victory of the stoic who, though the gods themselves crush him with superior weight, knows that his values are right and theirs wrong. The heroes of the great mock-epics are, by an ironical twist,

always more admirable, because more human, than the demi-gods
of true epic whom they parody. (26)

Burgess pits his protagonists against a gangster-God, thus
adding to the stature of his antiheroic figures. Those who fail
to engage in the contest, those who refuse to participate in the
Manichaean "great duality," are finally called "neutrals"; and
true evil is revealed in and by them. Because Burgess believes
that the world is temporarily in the hands of the wrong God,
organized religion receives a good deal of cynical comment. The
prison chaplain in *A Clockwork Orange* is constantly drunk;
Ambrose is a name frequently used to remind the reader of
the fourth-century bishop of Milan; and black masses are occasionally used to suggest the failure of religion. But then there
are eating and drinking scenes in many places that dictate an
opposing point of view. The Eucharist, taking God in the mouth,
is mentioned in many novels. Yet Burgess's protagonists are
constantly losing their dentures or having their teeth knocked
out. Surprisingly, a great deal of humor is occasioned by such
juxtapositions.

There are a number of sociological problems approached in
the novels. Social injustice, adultery, fidelity to nations and to
causes are themes that appear in almost all the books, but more
often than not these themes are subtly related to a religious
consideration. Allegorically, at times delicately but at others
somewhat belligerently, Burgess directs his reader to the theme
of guilt and responsibility.

Mood contrasts, tempo contrasts, musical frameworks, surrealistic descriptions, the experimenter's desire to discover new
modes of communication—Burgess indulges in all of these devices
to enlarge the dimensions of the novel. Surely his reputation as a
novelist will continue to grow, for he is one of the most important
English novelists to emerge in the second half of this century.

Notes and References

Chapter One

1. Anthony Burgess, *The Novel Now*: *A Guide to Contemporary Fiction* (New York, 1967), p. 213. Subsequent references are to this edition and will be included in the text.
2. Anthony Burgess, *A Vision of Battlements* (New York, 1966), p. vii. In a letter to the author dated March 20, 1968, Mr. Burgess wrote: "Myself as a musician am hard to fix chronologically. The works performed publicly are mostly incidental music to plays, orchestral works done by amateur and semi-professional orchestras, works pirated by Spanish radio. I still write music, and have had things as it were insinuated into literary programs on BBC television and used in poetry readings and so on. In other words, my music has to get in by the backdoor."
3. Anthony Burgess, "Letter from England," *The American Scholar*, XXXV (Spring, 1967), 263.
4. *Life*, LXV (October 25, 1968), 87-88. References are to this photo interview.
5. Anthony Lewis, "'I Love England, But I Will No Longer Live There,'" Interview with Burgess, *The New York Times Magazine*, November 3, 1968, pp. 38-40. Subsequent references are to this interview.
6. "Millions on a Musical About Shakespeare," *Times Saturday Review*, August 24, 1968, p. 18.
7. *Contemporary Authors III*, ed. James Etheredge (Detroit, n.d.).
8. Anthony Burgess, "The Manichean," *Times Literary Supplement*, no. 3340 (March 3, 1966), 154.
9. *Ibid.*, 153.
10. Anthony Burgess, "Letter from England," *The Hudson Review*, XIX (August, 1966), 455. Subsequent references to this essay will be included in the text.
11. Anthony Burgess, "An Electric Grape," *The American Scholar*, XXXV (Autumn, 1966), 719.
12. Anthony Burgess, "The Writer and Music," *The Listener*, LXVII (May 3, 1962), 761-62.

Chapter Two

1. Anthony Burgess, *The Novel Now*, p. 123. Subsequent references will be included in the text.

2. Anthony Burgess, "The Book Is Not for Reading," *The New York Times Book Review*, December 4, 1966, p. 1.

3. Anthony Burgess, *Re Joyce* (New York, 1966), p. 106.

4. Rex Warner, "The Allegorical Method," *The Cult of Power* (Philadelphia, 1947), p. 130. Subsequent references are to this edition and will be included in the text.

5. Anthony Burgess, *Language Made Plain* (London, 1964), p. 180.

6. Anthony Burgess, "Joyce Can't Really Be Imitated," *Books and Bookmen*, XV (July, 1970), 9.

7. Anthony Burgess, "The Seventeenth Novel," *The New York Times Book Review*, August 21, 1966, p. 2.

8. Richard B. Sewell, *The Vision of Tragedy* (New Haven, 1959), p. 110.

9. Martin D'Arcy, "The Anatomy of a Hero," *Transformation Three*, eds. Schimanski and Treece (London, n.d.), pp. 16-18.

10. Lewis Nichols, "Mr. Burgess," *The New York Times Book Review*, April 10, 1966, p. 8.

11. Anthony Burgess, Review of Mordecai Richler's *Cocksure*, *Life*, LXIV (March 15, 1968), 8.

Chapter Three

1. Anthony Burgess, *The Novel Now*, p. 211. Subsequent references will be included in the text.

2. Anthony Burgess, *A Vision of Battlements* (London, 1965), p. 8. Citations will be to this edition.

3. See the Ballantine edition of *A Vision of Battlements*, 1966.

4. Anthony Burgess, *The Long Day Wanes: A Malayan Trilogy* (New York, 1966). References are to the paperback edition and will be included in the text. The references to the various novels will be clearly marked. For fuller bibliographical information, the Bibliography should be consulted.

5. I am indebted to my colleague, Professor Sanford Goldstein, who searched out these meanings amongst his Indian students.

Chapter Four

1. Anthony Burgess, *The Right to an Answer* (New York, 1966). References are to the paperback edition. Fuller bibliographical information is included in the Bibliography.

2. Anthony Burgess, *The Novel Now*. Subsequent references will be included in the text.

3. Anthony Burgess, "Pronounced Vla-DEEM-ear Nah-BOAK-off," *The New York Times Book Review*, July 2, 1967, p. 20. Subsequent references to this review will be included in the text.

4. Anthony Burgess, *The Doctor Is Sick* (New York, 1967). References are to the paperback edition. Fuller bibliographical information is included in the Bibliography.

5. Burgess uses this observation significantly in several novels, especially in *One Hand Clapping*, where it assumes thematic importance.

6. Anthony Burgess, *Devil of a State* (New York, 1962). Subsequent references are to this edition. Fuller bibliographical information is included in the Bibliography.

7. Stanley Edgar Hyman (in "Afterword," in the Ballantine and Norton editions of *A Clockwork Orange*) suggests that there is no plot in the novel.

Chapter Five

1. Anthony Burgess, *The Worm and the Ring* (London, 1961). Subsequent references will be to this edition.

2. *The Times Literary Supplement*, Friday, July 7, 1961, p. 241, complained as follows, "There is not an atom of deep-down-goodness to be found in the leering, spotty, bullying school boys"; the *Times*, misunderstanding Burgess's purpose, complained too that the theme was not strikingly original. Somehow the reviewer missed the meaning of the novel.

3. Anthony Burgess, "The Politics of Graham Greene," *The New York Times Book Review*, September 10, 1967, p. 2. Subsequent references will be included in the text.

4. Anthony Burgess, *The Novel Now*, p. 39.

5. Anthony Burgess, *A Clockwork Orange* (New York, 1965). Subsequent references will be to this edition. Fuller bibliographical information is included in the Bibliography.

6. Anthony Burgess, *The Wanting Seed* (New York, 1964). Subsequent references will be to this edition. Fuller bibliographical information is included in the Bibliography.

7. Anthony Burgess, *A Clockwork Orange*. Subsequent references to the 1962 edition are specifically made in the text.

8. Julian Mitchell in "Reputation X: Anthony Burgess," *The London Magazine*, III (February, 1964), 54, points out that Burgess has incorporated Valéry's "Le Cimetière marin" into the closing lines of the novel.

Chapter Six

1. I am indebted to Mr. Burgess for this information.

2. Anthony Burgess, *The Novel Now*, p. 212.

3. Anthony Burgess, *One Hand Clapping* (London, 1961). Subsequent references are to this edition.

4. Anthony Burgess, *The Worm and the Ring*, p. 176.

5. Anthony Burgess, *Inside Mr. Enderby* (London, 1963). Subsequent references are to this edition.

6. Anthony Burgess, *Enderby Outside* (London, 1968). Subsequent references are to this edition.

Chapter Seven

1. Anthony Burgess, *Honey for the Bears* (New York, 1964). Subsequent references will be to this edition. The novel was written in the second half of 1961. Bibliographical information is included in the Bibliography.

2. See *America*, CX (February 8, 1964), 20; *Newsweek*, LXIII (February 3, 1964), 81; and the *Times Literary Supplement*, March 29, 1963, p. 213.

3. Christopher Ricks, "The Epicene," *New Statesman*, LXV (April 5, 1963), 496.

4. Several of the scenes evidently spring from Burgess's experience while traveling with his wife in Russia. See "Human Russians," *Science Digest*, LI (May, 1962), 33-37.

5. I am indebted to my student Miss Donna Clevinger for searching out these meanings for me in the *New Complete Russian-English Dictionary* (London, 1943).

6. Anthony Burgess, *Nothing Like the Sun* (New York, 1965). Subsequent references are to this edition. Fuller bibliographical information is included in the Bibliography.

7. Anthony Burgess, "Genesis and Headache," in *Afterwords*, ed. Thomas McCormack (New York, 1969). Subsequent references are to this edition.

8. Theodore Spencer, *Shakespeare and the Nature of Man* (New York, 1949), p. 94.

9. Anthony Burgess, *The Eve of St. Venus* (London, 1964). Subsequent references are to this edition. *The Eve of St. Venus*, Mr. Burgess wrote to the author on Easter Tuesday, 1968, was scheduled to be staged in London in 1968.

10. Anthony Burgess, *Tremor of Intent* (New York, 1966). Subsequent references are to this edition. Fuller bibliographical information is included in the Bibliography.

11. García Lorca, *Bodas de sangre*, Act IV. I am indebted to my student Mrs. LaVerne Gonzalez for this excellent translation.

Chapter Eight

1. Anthony Burgess, *Re Joyce* (New York, 1966), p. 23. Subsequent references will be to this edition. Fuller bibliographical information is included in the Bibliography.

Selected Bibliography

PRIMARY SOURCES

1. Major Works

Listed below are Anthony Burgess's published books. The facts of
American hard cover publication are listed in parentheses. In several
cases the dates of both British and American publication are the same.

Time for a Tiger. London: Heinemann, 1956.
The Enemy in the Blanket. London: Heinemann, 1958.
Beds in the East. London: Heinemann, 1958.
English Literature: A Survey for Students. (As John Burgess Wilson)
London: Longmans, 1958.
The Right to an Answer. London: Heinemann, 1958.
The Doctor Is Sick. London: Heinemann, 1960. (New York: Norton,
1961).
Devil of a State. London: Heinemann, 1961. (New York: Norton,
1966).
One Hand Clapping. (As Joseph Kell) London: Peter Davies, 1961.
The Worm and the Ring. London: Heinemann, 1961.
The Wanting Seed. London: Heinemann, 1962. (New York: Norton,
1964).
A Clockwork Orange. London: Heinemann, 1962. (New York: Nor-
ton, 1963).
Inside Mr. Enderby. (As Joseph Kell) London: Heinemann, 1963.
(Included in *Enderby*. New York: Norton, 1968).
Honey for the Bears. London: Heinemann, 1963. (New York: Nor-
ton, 1964).
The Novel Today. British Council Pamphlet. The British Council, 1963.
Malayan Trilogy. London: Heinemann, 1963. Includes *Time for a
Tiger, The Enemy in the Blanket, Beds in the East*. (Entitled
The Long Day Wanes. New York: Norton, 1965).
The Eve of St. Venus. London: Sidgwick, 1964.
Language Made Plain. London: English Universities Press, 1964.
Nothing Like the Sun. London: Heinemann, 1964. (New York:
Norton, 1964).
*Here Comes Everybody: An Introduction to James Joyce for the
Ordinary Reader*. London: Faber, 1965. (Entitled *Re Joyce*.
New York: Norton, 1965).

Tremor of Intent. London: Heinemann, 1965. (New York: Norton, 1965).

A Vision of Battlements. London: Sidgwick, 1965. (New York: Norton, 1965).

A Shorter Finnegans Wake. (Edition of Joyce's *Finnegans Wake*). London: Faber, 1966. (New York: Viking, 1966).

Enderby Outside. London: Heinemann, 1968. (*Enderby*, New York: Norton, 1968. Includes *Inside Mr. Enderby* and *Enderby Outside*).

Urgent Copy. New York: Norton, 1968. Contains the following articles and essays that first appeared in periodicals, magazines, and newspapers: 1. The Greene and the Red: Politics in the Novels of Graham Greene; Waugh Begins; The Comedy of Ultimate Truths; Dark Disease: A European Tradition. 2. The First Madame Bovary; Dickens Loud and Clear; The Brotherhood; The Answerer; Gash Gold-Vermilion. 3. Enemy of Twilight; Cast a Cold Eye: The Yeats Centenary; The Two Shaws; The Perfect Shavian; Dear Mr. Shame's Voice; Shem the Penman; *Ulysses*: How Well Has It Worn; Enduring Saturday; The Writer as Drunk; Man and Artist: Homage to Dylan. 4. Lewis as Spaceman; Lament for a Maker; Kipling and the Kuch-Nays; Kipling: A Celebration in Silence; Said Rudyard to Rider. 5. Making the White Boss Frown; He Wrote Good; The Postwar American Novel: A View from the Periphery; The Jew as American; Blood in the Matzos; Caprine Messiah; Poet and Pedant. 6. Koestler's Danube; Treasures and Fetters; What Now in the Novel?. 7. In Search of Shakespeare the Man; Dr. Rowstus; The Milton Revolution; Bagehot on Books; The Democracy of Prejudice; The Steinerian Agony; A Very Tragic Business; *Fleurs du Mal*; The Triple Thinker. 8. Graves and Omar; On English in English; English as an America; Word, World and Meaning; The Proper Study of Literary Man; Snow White and Rose Red. 9. The Good Companion; The Modicum is the Message; What is Pornography?; If Oedipus had read his Lévi-Strauss; Why All this Fuss about Librairies?; Epilogue; Conflict and Confluence.

Shakespeare. London: Jonathan Cape, 1970. (New York: Knopf, 1970).

2. Stories, Essays, Articles, and Reviews

"Anatomy of Melancholy," *Horizon*, XII (August, 1970), 48-53.

"The Book Is Not for Reading," *The New York Times Book Review*, December 4, 1966, p. 1, 74.

"Daltonian Prejudice," *Guardian*, November 16, 1966, p. 20.

"Dear Mr. Shame's Voice," *The Spectator*, CCXIII (November 27, 1964), 731. Reprinted in *Atlas*, X (July, 1965), 51-53. See "Joyce Industry in the United States."

"Democracy of Prejudice," *Encounter*, XXIX (February, 1967), 67-71.

"Did Shakespeare Mean That, or Is It A Printer's Error," *Chicago Tribune*, January 12, 1969, p. 5.

"Doctor Rouse Meets Doctor Faustus," *Nation*, CC (February 1, 1965), 115 ff. Review of *Christopher Marlowe*.

"An Electric Grape," *The American Scholar*, XXV (Autumn, 1966), 719-20.

"English as an America," *Encounter*, XXVIII (February, 1967), 67-71.

"Genesis and Headache," in *Afterwords: Novelists on Their Novels*, ed. Thomas McCormack. New York: Harper and Row, 1969.

"Gibraltar," *Holiday*, XLI (February, 1967), 70-71.

"A Good Man Destroyed—Hilariously," *Life*, LXIV (March 15, 1968), 8. Review of *Cocksure*.

"Great Mogul Beethoven," *Vogue*, CLV (March 15, 1970), 132-33.

"Great Vowel Shift and All That," *Encounter*, XXVI (May, 1966), 70-73.

"The Human Russians," *The Listener*, LVI (December 28, 1961), 1106-8. Reprinted in *Science Digest*, LI (May, 1962), 33-37.

"Joyce Can't Really Be Imitated," *Books and Bookmen*, XV (July, 1970), 8-9.

"Joyce Industry in the United States," *Atlas*, X (July, 1965), 51-53. Reprint of *Spectator* article of November 27, 1964 entitled "Dear Mr. Shame's Voice."

"Language, Myth, and Mr. Updike," *Commonweal*, LXXXIII (February 11, 1966), 557-59. Comments on Updike's art; review of *On the Farm*.

"Letter from England," *The American Scholar*, XXXVI (Spring, 1967), 261-65.

"Letter from Europe," *The American Scholar*, XXXVIII (Spring, 1969), 297-99.

"Letter from Europe," *The American Scholar*, XXXVIII (Winter, 1969), 104-9.

"Letter from Europe," *The American Scholar*, XXXIX (Summer, 1970), 502-4.

"Letter from Europe," *The American Scholar*, XL (Winter, 1970), 119-22.

"London Letter," *The American Scholar*, XXVI (Autumn, 1967), 636-38.

"London Letter," *The American Scholar*, XXVIII (Spring, 1968), 312-15.

"Letter from England," *The Hudson Review*, XIX (August, 1966), 455-60.

"London Letter," *The Hudson Review*, XX (Spring, 1967), 99-105.

"Letter from England," *The Hudson Review*, XX (Autumn, 1967), 454-58.

"Making de White Boss Frown," *Encounter*, XXVII (July, 1966), 54-58. Comments on *Uncle Tom's Cabin*.

"The Manicheans," *The Times Literary Supplement*, no. 3340 (March 3, 1966), 153-55.

"The Muse: A Sort of SF Story," *The Hudson Review*, XXI (Spring, 1968), 109-26. Science fiction; return to Shakespeare's England.

"Our Bedfellow, the Marquis de Sade," *Horizon*, XI (Winter, 1969), 104-9.

"The Politics of Graham Greene," *The New York Times Book Review*, September 10, 1967, p. 2.

"The Postwar American Novel," *The American Scholar*, XXV (Winter, 1965-66), 150-56.

"Powers That Be," *Encounter*, XXIV (January, 1965), 71-76.

"The Writer's Purpose," *The New York Times Book Review*, May 1, 1966, p. 2.

"Pronounced Vla-DEEM-ear Nah-BOAK-off," *The New York Times Book Review*, July 2, 1967, p. 1, 20. Review of Andrew Field's *Nabokov: His Life in Art*.

"Reading Your Own," *The New York Times Book Review*, June 4, 1967, p. 6.

"Seeing the Shape of Things to Come," *The New York Times Book Review*, August 3, 1969, p. 1 ff. Review of *H. G. Wells*, by Lovat Dickson.

"Seen Any Good Galsworthy Lately?" *The New York Times Magazine*, November 16, 1968, p. 57.

"The Seventeenth Novel," *The New York Times Book Review*, August 21, 1967, p. 2, 14.

"Speaking of Writing," *Times*, January 16, 1964, p. 13.

"Vieux Chapeau," *The New York Times Book Review*, March 3, 1968, pp. 4-5. Review of *Les Belles Images*.

"Work and Play," *The New York Times Book Review*, June 5, 1966, p. 1.

"The Writer and Music," *The Listener*, LXVII (May 3, 1962), 761-62.

SECONDARY SOURCES

ADLER, DICK. "Inside Mr. Burgess," *Sunday Times Magazine*, April 2, 1967, pp. 47-50. Comments on Burgess's themes and values in his art.

AGGELER, GEOFFREY. "The Comic Art of Anthony Burgess," *Arizona Quarterly*, XXV (Autumn, 1969), 234-51. A survey of Burgess's novels best known in the United States; emphasis on their originality.

CLEMENS, WALTER. "Anthony Burgess: Pushing On," *The New York Times Book Review,* November 29, 1970, p. 2. Comments on Burgess's stay in United States; his plans for future writing.

HICKS, GRANVILLE. "The Fertile World of Anthony Burgess," *Saturday Review,* L (July 15, 1967), 27-29. Comments on Burgess's desire to experiment: "he has a lively mind, a merciless gift for satire, stylistic originality of an extraordinary range, and a creative drive without parallel in our own time."

HORDER, JOHN. "Art That Pays," *Guardian,* October 10, 1964, p. 5.

HYMAN, STANLEY EDGAR. "Anthony Burgess," *On Contemporary Literature,* ed. Richard Kostelanetz. New York: Avon, 1964, pp. 33-305. Reprinted as an Afterword in the Norton and Ballantine editions. Portions of Mr. Hyman's text appeared earlier in *The New Leader,* for which he was an editor. Includes a glossary of Nadsat terms used in the novel. Comments on the thematic development of *A Clockwork Orange.*

MITCHELL, JULIAN. "Reputations—X: Anthony Burgess," *The London Magazine,* III (February, 1964), 48-54. "[T]his despair at man's inability to improve himself, at his incompetence and lack of moral nerve, underlies all the comedies of the novels." Calls Crabbe's guilt "old-fashioned."

NICHOLS, LEWIS. "Mr. Burgess," *The New York Times Book Review,* April 10, 1966, p. 8. Recounts interview with Burgess about works and views of literature.

PRITCHARD, W. H. "The Novels of Anthony Burgess," *Massachusetts Review,* VII (Summer, 1966), 525-39. Says that Burgess's characters are viewed "externally as ever, and their dimensions (and our sympathies) are thus severely limited."

RICKS, CHRISTOPHER. "The Epicene," *New Statesman,* LXV (April 5, 1963), 496. Ostensibly a review of *Honey for the Bears,* but bears on all the novels. "Russia turns out to be disconcertingly like America . . . so that politically the book is about a Third Force that will combine and outdo them."

SULLIVAN, WALTER. "Death Without Tears: Anthony Burgess and the Dissolution of the West," *The Hollins Critic,* VI (April, 1969), 1-11. A survey of the novels. "One of the points Burgess makes is that humanity is all of a piece. And if, as he sets forth, Hindus and Buddhists and Muslims have a claim to truth and virtue equal to that of the Christian, then they must also accept the same taint of evil."

Index

85090